Fathers and Sons

Fathers and Sons

EDITED BY JOHN HOYLAND

For Liz

Library of Congress Catalog Card Number: 91-61206

British Library Cataloguing-in-Publication Data
Fathers and sons.
I. Hoyland, John
306.874

ISBN 1-85242-203-3

First published 1992 by Serpent's Tail,
4 Blackstock Mews, London N4, and
401 West Broadway #2, New York, NY 10012

Typeset in 11/13½pt Sabon by Contour Typesetters, Southall, London
Printed in Great Britain by
Cox & Wyman Ltd. of Reading, Berkshire

CONTENTS

INTRODUCTION

He cuddles us in his arms, holds us up high above the ground. He is very large and very strong, and when he kisses us his face is almost unbearably rough. For some of us, he is the only man who will ever cuddle us and kiss us, the only man who will show us physical love.

We are very aware of his strength. There is a hardness about him that is different from what we feel with the mother. This hardness can be very protective, but it also makes us aware of his separateness from us.

As time goes on, our sense of his separateness grows. We become aware of his absences, of his involvement in a world we do not know about – the world outside the home. We notice that his rhythms and his moods, even his smells, are conditioned by this other world. There is something alien about him, a sense in which he is a stranger. He is driven by a force we do not understand.

This strangeness can perplex us, but it is also very impressive – so much so that he can appear almost like a god to us. We go through a time of hero-worshipping him. We learn the stories of his triumphs and his adventures in the world. The stories become myths, exaggerated by both father and son. We believe there is nothing he cannot do, that his ability to control his destiny and ours is limitless.

We are in awe of him – and, almost certainly, we also fear him. He may seem godlike in his power and wisdom, and perhaps in his goodness, but he can also be terrible in his readiness to control us and in his dispensation of justice. For many, in fact, he is a tyrant more than a god – a tyrant whose will must not be challenged, whose rage must not be provoked.

Just the same, there will be times when we resist his authority. He has probably taught us himself about the importance of fairness, yet often we feel he is not fair. So we fight him back, and risk his rage. We start to develop a sense of having a will of our own in opposition to his, and a conflict is born from which we may never completely free ourselves.

There may be times, too, when his rage is turned against the mother, when he appears to make her unhappy, when he seems different, or less, than what she wants. At such times he can become a monster, a person who is hard and unfeeling and cold. Desiring to protect the mother from him, we may even come to dread his disruptive presence in the home.

For some of us, at quite an early age, this dread can be mixed with scorn. The god fails us early on. Though we still fear him, he is diminished for us. And if, like many fathers, he retreats from the domestic battleground – into introspection, or drink, or simple absence – we may even come to see him as an irrelevance and an oddity.

But then there are times when he suddenly becomes our companion and our friend. He plays with us, wrestles with us, shares adventures with us. He tells us his jokes and his stories. He introduces us to his male pleasures, taking us fishing or to his favourite sport, showing us the things he loves and that make him feel free. He even becomes mischievous, making us feel we are in a gang with him, sharing the illicit thrills of breaking rules and getting into trouble.

We feel drawn into an alliance with him, an alliance of free spirits against authority – or an alliance of men against women.

Our happiest moments with him can be when he steps down

from his Olympian heights like this – when he, too, becomes a boy.

But frequently he does none of these things, because, quite simply, he isn't there. For much of the time he is absent. And often, even when he is there, he ignores us. So we spend much of our childhood striving to make him recognise us, to make him notice us and commend us. Our actions are only half complete until he has given them his approval.

For whether he is a god or a tyrant or a friend, he always retains a certain power. So we come to think that our quest in life as boys, and then as men, is to discover the source of this power – to understand and appropriate its mystery.

We will spend the rest of our lives on this quest, and it will always be bound up in our minds with winning the father's approval. We know we have to deliver for him. We have to justify his confidence and love; we have to avoid his displeasure and scorn; we have to live up to what he seems to want of us; we have to show that we can do it too.

Even if our quest takes the form of a rebellion against him and what he stands for, he is still the measure of it.

So we learn that it is shameful to cry, even when he beats us. We learn to keep our feelings in check, so that emotions will not deflect us from our quest. We learn that to be powerful like him, we must be in control.

And we learn, too, that there is a continuity in all this. We become aware of the male line of inheritance, the line that stretches from the grandfather through the father down to us. There is something magical in this inheritance, just as there is something magical in the father's power. In learning to be men, we are learning to take our place in the magical line.

What we seldom know, at this time in our boyhood, is that his power is limited, and that he, too, longs for success, fame, vigour, romance, wealth, certainty. He, too, fears that he may not measure up to what is wanted. He, too, is frustrated in his ambitions, fears that he may have failed. He, too, experiences shame.

Sometimes, when he shares his dreams with us, they lift us up, as we glimpse with him the beckoning of the infinitely possible. But when we glimpse his frustrations, we are appalled. We cannot bear to think that he has anything less than total free will.

His achievements are our achievements, and his failures are ours also.

Do these generalisations apply to all of us, even to any of us?

I cannot know, for sure. There is certainly a sense in which they do not apply to me. My father was killed when I was very young, and editing and contributing to this book has been, in part, a search for him and what he has meant to me. Equally, for some of the other writers here, the father was such a distant figure that a relationship with him hardly existed at all.

Yet patterns of sonhood seem to emerge. And I feel a sufficient identity with the other sons who write here to feel that, yes, each of us is conditioned by a relationship that is particular to us, but we are still united by these relationships into some kind of 'we'.

One of the father's roles that many of the writers here refer to is the role of teacher. When the son becomes an adolescent, especially, we find the father wanting to pass on his skills, and with them his view of the world.

We sons may resist some of this from a developing sense that the father's skills are not necessarily the same as ours. But we also want to please him, as always. So we feel the greatest wretchedness when we believe we are failing in his eyes – and nothing makes us more fulfilled than when we sense that he is proud of us and what we do. His acknowledgment that we are getting the hang of things can be the first sign that there might be a mutuality between us and him, that there might be ways in which we are equal beings.

But there is another side to this maturing. As we get to know more about the world ourselves, we become more aware of the father's weaknesses. We learn more and more that there are limits to his will, that there are things he cannot do and things he is not good at. Even his achievements begin to seem smaller to us, as we focus more on what we want to achieve ourselves.

The discovery that he is imperfect and vulnerable makes us realise that perhaps, after all, he is not so unlike ourselves. This can draw us to him. But it can also mean that, more seriously than ever before, we begin to question his authority.

At the same time, we notice the ways in which we are different from him. We realise that to become a man may be less to do with being like him than with being individuals in our own right. Sometimes, we feel so different from him that it seems extraordinary that we have lived in such proximity to him for so long.

He can even begin to seem a little comic to us. We are no longer impressed by his experience. Now it alienates us, even seems absurd. He belongs to a different generation. He is old-fashioned. We feel he cannot understand us, and never will.

We realise how much of our relationship with him is a matter of obligation. We continue to perform the role of sons, but the role now seems empty to us. We no longer want to talk to him about what we are doing and feeling. We don't want him to contaminate the autonomous selves that we are struggling to build.

We find ourselves feeling stifled by him. He holds us back from being what we want to be.

11

So a time comes when we have to fight him.

We have to defeat him, be free of him. We have to separate from him, and go our own way.

This battle of wills may be a sporadic or muted one, or it may be so prolonged and fierce that the relationship hardly recovers from it. But either way, the separation takes place eventually. The father lets the son go. The son becomes free.

And then, when the wounds begin to heal, when we have struck out on our own, a time comes when we begin to relate to the father in a new way – as man to man. We start to drink together, perhaps; we discuss problems of politics or work with something approaching equality; perhaps we even talk about more personal things.

There can be a great feeling of arrival when this happens. It is what we have longed for – the recognition, from the one person who can give it, that we, too, are adult men.

This is especially the case when we have children of our own. It is a moment when the relationship between father and son can shift dramatically. On the one hand, in continuing the line of inheritance (whether to sons or daughters), we have provided one of the greatest possible fulfilments of the father's expectations of us. On the other hand, in becoming fathers ourselves, we break something of the mystique that has obscured the father's human reality from us.

But for many of us, even now, the equality is incomplete. Parts of our relationship with him have become frozen along the way. Parts of us still believe he can handle things, or at least that he ought to do so. Parts of us still want to impress him, or detach ourselves from him, or contradict him. Parts of us are still the admiring, rebelling child – the son.

How many of our childhood heroes and tyrants really become our friends?

How many of them learn to talk to us of themselves?

Often, the father's remoteness never really breaks down. And we, still a little in awe, still alienated by generational strangeness, never tell him of our love, never say, with John Fowles: "My father my father do not die."

When such moments of tenderness do occur, they often confuse us, but they are also particularly precious to us. For something else is happening now. We have seen that he is vulnerable like ourselves; we have seen that he can fail. But what we have not really anticipated is that he is also fragile – that he will grow old and infirm, and that he will die.

Perhaps it is only then, when the father grows frail, that we finally become men in our own eyes. We realise that from now on it is going to be up to us. We cannot expect him to do it for us any more.

And then he dies – and whether we have loved him or hated him, admired him or despised him, fought him or been his friend, when he dies a part of us dies with him. We are left with a particular kind of aloneness.

If we are no longer doing things for him, then what are we doing them for? And how can we survive, without his protection?

His death also teaches us that we, too, must die. Is there any consolation for this bitter truth?

The consolation offered by these sons writing about their fathers is summed up most simply, it seems to me, in the words spoken by the old man in the cemetery at the end of David Simon's story:

'A man can only inherit love; everyt'ing else jus' crumble.'

John Hoyland

13

MY INHERITANCE

DAVID SIMON

Under a hot colonial sun my grandfather took his old worn Bible that he had inherited, then uttered the words, 'Trust no man', before naming my father Samson. Many years later, draped in a heavy winter coat, Samson, who I called Daddy, took the same Bible, uttered the same words, and named me David: perhaps so that I would stand up for myself, even if it meant defeating giants. This was the story that Daddy repeatedly told me in his more sombre moods; it wasn't true, but it was his way of trying to tell me that the world was more cruel than any little child, as I was then, could possibly imagine.

Daddy was a man that I feared and loved; a man of immeasurable charm and spite; a man that I adored when he played sweet parang on his Spanish guitar; a man that I sometimes wanted to strike down with my legendary sling when I saw him bully my family. Yes, a big man made from the rainbow of races inhabiting the West Indies, who fraternised with beautiful women and low level politicians from the islands. He was a gentleman, yet he had been brought up to believe that life was a dog-fight: you took some blows, and you gave some too; and if your mouth was bloody, you didn't cry; you dusted your pants and cursed the next man that got in your way. Because of this apparent contradiction in his character, it took me over thirty years to understand him, and in that long and tearful journey, I came to understand the shame of manhood and my inheritance.

Perhaps I had too many feelings towards him; feelings that I would later question after I realised that I judged him and not the times he lived in, not the miserable world that made him finally fall upon his knees and weep. It is too late to say he could have been a good man; he was a good man, but good men in a bad world become pitiful bad men, whilst the world pretends to sing with goodness. I was his silent witness, who he never saw, who he never heard when I too cried.

I was the youngest boy, then, unaware of those so-called swinging sixties; his favourite, who he tickled with his Anancy stories one moment, then became oblivious to my need for love the next, when he became a man obsessed with mad passions for fame and money. It wasn't until many years later, in the year of '83, by which time that sun had gone from his smile, and his fingers could no longer hold that sweet guitar, that our relationship seemed to become important to him as well as me. In the summer of that year, now both men – I, the age he was when he first stepped from the boat-train, and he, an old man – we became angry and almost unforgiving towards each other. He knew that I was old enough to make a damning judgement upon his life; that buried in my youthful silence had been a critical memory, recalling key moments in the fiery relationships he had with those around him. I wanted to know why he made everyone buckle under the onslaught of his temper. Hadn't he travelled to get work, a house and education for us, his nine children? What made him continue ruthlessly? Was it because he was a man, and a man of colour, living in a world that denied him status and rights, making him snatch at impossible theories of how to achieve, of how to become the big man, the big man that perhaps would one day make history? How could Samson be the strongest man on earth with such a burden?

My first memory of Daddy was of him in '63 drinking rum; rum because he was a man from Carriacou, Carriacou that made strong rum and strong men; men that could drink one full glass straight; men that slapped one another on the back, laughed so that God himself could hear. This was the man that bounced me on his knee, measuring me with his fatherly eye, whose look somehow contained the belief that I would some day inherit something that he was building. I knew it wasn't just a house, or his land and goats back home, but something magical. I wanted to be like him; to have his broad smile and shoulders, his muscular arms that had built houses in Trinidad, lifted oil barrels in Aruba; but most of all, I wanted to play his guitar and sing like he did. I can remember, after cousins with baggy suits and gold in their teeth had come to the house, as he saw them to the door, how I sneaked a glass of his favourite brand of rum, Jack Iron. I tried to stand and drink it like him; then I went to his guitar to pluck it. At that age, five or so, I was in total awe of him, but I sensed that my older brothers and sisters weren't, that they knew something about our inheritance that I didn't.

One evening, tangled in play and day-dreams, I saw Daddy take a glass of his Jack Iron. I remember how his face grimaced, then how he became melancholy. It was the anniversary of his mother's death, the day that we weren't allowed to sing in the house, the day that he went to church, and the evening that he lit candles, placing several on the mantelpiece, watching the flames as he talked to the memory of the woman that had brought him into the world. His voice was unusually soft, displaying both weakness, fear and sensitivity. I remember him saying the words: 'T'ings hard in England, don't judge me yet.'

It was then, though I didn't comprehend fully, that I began to realise that Daddy didn't quite understand the world, that his mighty strength sought help from the supernatural. It was the first time I saw a man's tears. It made me scared of life. And hiding under our old gramophone that he used to play his Jim Reeves records, I kept still, not wanting him to find me, knowing that he would hide his hurt behind an explosion of anger that might see him take out his old leather belt. Even at that age I knew I wasn't supposed to see this – that men, especially those from Carriacou, had a private world that was never talked about or even admitted.

The very next day, a Monday that saw him stay home from work for no apparent reason other than sadness, he called all the children together to sit on the floor at his slippered feet, then began to tell us about Carriacou. Why, because in these moments of honesty and sadness he admitted to himself that he couldn't build his dream in England. He told us, as he had done several times before, that Carriacou was where our grandparents were buried; that Carriacou was near heaven; that Carriacou was a place of white sands and blue sea and hurricanes; a place where blue letters went and came from; a place where women wore big church hats and white frocks. He told us this so that we would be aware that we had an option in life, because his dream was being crushed by the outside world, preventing him from leaving us our inheritance. It puzzled us because on so many other occasions he mocked Carriacou for its smallness, then praised the opportunities that England now presented us with. So we were aware of this contradiction, but none of us were really old enough to dwell upon it. Who knew at that time how weak Samson was?

By the mid-sixties there were nine children, made in homes on either side of the Atlantic as Daddy travelled in search of work. Now we were living in a big Victorian house in south-east London, a house full of cobwebbed rooms and creaky stairs, but thankfully Mummy made it home. Within weeks it was full of cousins and friends from Carriacou, kissing us on the cheek, studying our features as they remembered our family from way back. These were the people that Daddy competed with: he had to have a bigger home, and car and family than they. And we, the children, had to do better in school than their children did. They were happy people, naive people, serious and hardworking people, church people, rum people, big hearted people, and there were the ridiculous people.

Already feeling that I was better than their children, perhaps I competed even more to make him realise that I existed. We were to become doctors, lawyers and teachers.

But there were times, mad, crazy and speculative times; days when I awoke to find the house full of excitement. Daddy had a new project; a way to make us rich. Suddenly his imagination was fired; he seemed to join me in my childhood, and would even unwittingly confide in me as he talked to himself about his crazy scheme. Activity and industry were all about, because Cousin Quashie, an ugly man with a nasty smile, had come to him with a joint business venture. Daddy and Cousin Quashie were to manufacture and sell batik curtains. Each morning he rose with his entrepreneural spirit, and each morning I joined him. Against the wishes of Mummy, the attic was turned into a factory. The smell of chemicals now filled the house. The rest of the family turned against Daddy, except for me because it was the one time he really talked to me. Unfortunately, the venture failed, like all previous ones, for the dye ran faster than Cousin Quashie who fled with some of Daddy's money. It left debt and public humiliation that Mummy and my older brothers and sister felt more than I.

It was about that time when I began to hear the secret conversations in the house about what my father was doing to the family. I soon realised that it wasn't only the family's reputation that he had squandered, but his savings too. After the incident it became painful to see him try to laugh and charm his way out of the humiliation. Now, when I looked into the eyes of cousins I'd been told I was better than, they seemed to have pity in their eyes. They continued to laugh and drink, and play cards and dominoes with him, but I was aware of pretence for the first time, and aware too of the increasing heaviness of his burden that he never spoke about.

As the years went by he became suspicious of me, not trusting me with any of his secrets because I was old enough to show an opinion, even if it was only a disapproving look. Now, when he had an idea he didn't tell anyone else in the family; a relative or friend would come running to tell Mummy, who, in turn, would come, with humiliation once again chasing her, to tell us. And these embarrassing tales might be about Daddy loaning money to irresponsible individuals with big grins, or, about another badly organised coach trip that would leave him in debt.

On one occasion we heard that Daddy had formed 'The Carriacou Benevolent and Philanthropic Society', a venture aimed at raising money for the people back home and raising Daddy's profile in the local community. A grand dance was then organised at Greenwich Town Hall. We, the children, were told by Daddy to sell tickets to our friends. He used our heads as calculators, telling us to work out financial sums that would prove that he was going to become rich. Whether we liked it or not, and we never did, we suddenly found ourselves reluctantly part of this fiasco. As usual, the night before the dance things went wrong. The old calypso band that he had booked against better judgement, had broken up acrimoniously over the love of a woman from Dominica; the DJ had had his record box stolen; tickets had been returned unsold, and the Management Committee of the hall had informed Daddy that they kept all profits of the bar. I can remember Daddy trying on his new tuxedo when the phone calls came to pass on this information. Immediately he became angry. He blamed Trinidadians for inventing calypso and irresponsible musicians; he blamed my little sister's first year mathematics for the miscalculations on the bar. He blamed everyone other than himself. I didn't know whether to laugh or cry. The next thing we knew his contingency plan suddenly made us all important again. Suddenly trust was back in our relationship. I was to be the new DJ. He hadn't taken into account that I only had ten records. Thrilled, I revelled in this delegation, because, in a way it seemed to prove that he had an opinion of me to hand me such a responsible job at thirteen. Next, Danny, my eldest brother, who was a singer in a soul band, was told to put on a flowered shirt and sing calypso at the dance. My sisters were also forced into being the caterers, and spent the whole night cooking roties and curry goat. After all this, the dance flopped. Daddy blamed the family, especially me for playing the same ten records. His ridicule hurt. He ended up having to work lots of overtime to pay off the debts that the grand dance left him in and to keep the Society afloat, he took back the housekeeping money from Mummy.

Now, in the seventies, I lived in a house of a broken marriage; Mummy slept in one room, Daddy, in another. Whenever he did something that he shouldn't have done, he came to me guiltily, trying to ease his conscience and win back a little of the love that he knew he was losing. It was at this time that I realised who he was; that all his life he had see-sawed between being strong and weak; that, at times he had devoted himself to the family, but when things got too bad he fled into long moods of anger and self-pity. It was at this time, as I left school to work that I began to realise that he had lived two lives; that he hadn't simply been the man of dreams, but each day he had had to go out to work, to be a postman, to keep posting letters to feed his ambitions and his family. Was he really paranoid or was Carriacou telling him to be something whilst this strange society he had come to live in kept repeatedly laughing at his struggle? But soon I gained a sympathy for Daddy that I didn't quite understand myself when I too was faced with the same world.

We had now become two different men. Because of his ill health I was now stronger than Samson, but, as I came to know him, I would perhaps realise that he had left me an inheritance after all.

I graduated in '83, reaching an age when I wanted to intellectualise upon the world, blaming his generation for making the independence movements of the black diaspora fail. Even in our moments of silence when I took him to hospital there was anger between us; he, feeling that I hadn't realised what he had been through, whilst I felt that he hadn't realised what the family had had to endure. By this time he was broken, though he didn't want to admit it, because the woman whom he had loved sporadically for over three-quarters of his life had left him; all his children were big and relieved to be away from the humiliation. And the big old house that he had bought had been sold. Each week I found myself visiting him out of pity and guilt. He was old now. Arthritis had set in in the legs that once walked the London streets, and his elbows no longer allowed him to bang down the winning domino. Those that he had once counselled about house buying and marriage, no longer came to see him in his medicine-littered home.

His confidantes have become the priest and doctor, both of whom have forbidden him to drink his Jack Iron. His loneliness hurts me, more than it hurts him. And most of his friends, those men from Carriacou who slapped one another on their backs, are dead now. Each time I visit him I listen to his sad soliloquy, that eventually meanders into a disturbing confession. On some occasions I find him reading his Bible, a book he now knows well. I never try and make him expose more of his feelings than he wants to, even if I think it might be therapeutic, because I know that he still remembers the words his grandfather told him: 'Trust no man!' Or, perhaps it was because he had never learnt to express his feelings: to do so would be to discover another side of himself, and people become lazy out of fear to discover something new about life. So we sit quietly in his room, listening to the radio, bathed in sunlight that lances in through the netted curtains. Occasionally he tries to explain his actions of the past, knowing that I want answers to why he did the things he did. He always starts: '. . . A man has to decide . . . A man must put him foot down . . .' His tone is still stubborn and defiant. Each time I leave him there is more sympathy and guilt inside me, as I realise the true weight of the burden he'd been carrying all these years. And slowly I began to realise that to know this man I had to know from where he came.

It was in the summer of '83 that I left England to make my pilgrimage to Carriacou, knowing that I was going to trespass on Daddy's history, most of which he didn't want me to see. I found myself sailing on a fisherman's boat to Carriacou, having just left revolutionary Grenada. Already, in my mind, I could hear Daddy putting down the government of Maurice Bishop; not because of politics, but because Daddy had played cricket with the leader of the opposition party.

The sky was clear, the sun was hot and the sea temperamental; the swaying boat was packed with shoppers returning from the mainland. At this time I saw everything through the eyes of a romantic. These were Daddy's people, full of stories and jokes: but, as time went by, I would see these people eating just one meal a day; I would hear their prayers in church. I would watch their endless labour. They were poor. Had Daddy been as poor as them? Guilt insisted on returning; mocking me, the young graduate, when I took out my note pad and pen, believing that I would one day write a book about them.

I began to hear Daddy's beautiful parang songs as I looked out in the distance and saw a small idyllic island. When I first saw this picture of white sands and majestic swaying palms, I naively asked myself: why had Daddy left all this? By this time, still in the boat, people had come up to me with a smile and asked: 'You is Samson bwoy?' As I smiled, squinting and having further studied my features, they'd say: 'Yeah man, you have him nose; all Samson family have nose dat stay big.' After this they'd talk about Daddy and Mummy; about how they were when they were young. It made me proud and sentimental, but then their expressions would turn bitter as they looked into the sea slapping against the side of the boat. I knew that they knew that something had gone wrong, but I felt that they couldn't articulate it any better than me or Daddy. They simply accepted it as life, but I didn't. On the wharf, waiting with smiles and tears, was my aunt, who I had never seen, but she immediately recognised this strange black Englishman with his big nose and box of breadfruit; a gift to greet her welcome.

Perhaps, because she knew this was a pilgrimage, the very next day she gave me a two bottles; one containing rum, the other containing water. She told me where my grandfather's grave was, then sent me on my way to pay my respects as old customs demanded. It was the rainy season; it had just poured, so there was an unreal freshness all about. As I continued, I came to an old church that I assumed was now derelict. Walking by I began hearing the reciting of school-children, so I came off the dirt track road, walking along a small path flanked with shrubs, and looked through the broken window of the church. To my surprise there were dozens of small children crammed into this one little classroom sitting on the floor with slates and chalk. Their eyes and mouths were open, eagerly taking in everything they could. In front of them was a young school teacher with a small blackboard. There was no doubt in my mind that this school was old enough to have been the one that Daddy had studied in; that he left when he was thirteen; the same school that he used to tell me that he wished he could have stayed on longer in. Already I could hear his words from years gone by: 'Bwoy, study your book, you hear!' I hadn't understood when he flogged us when we brought home a bad report, or why he kept buying improve-yourself books. But now I did.

I continued to walk, half worried that there would be another downpour, while at the same time observing the beautiful wild flowers that Daddy had once picked and brought to my mother waiting on her veranda. It was when I came across a tiny house, probably built on a foundation that had held many houses before it, that I realised I was lost. A few noisy fowls in the yard announced my arrival. A voice called to me. An old woman with wet hands and a chuckle in her throat, parted her tatty washing that hung in the yard.

'You is foreigner?' I told her I was Samson's son. A smile came to her face; she began to sing one of his songs that he'd composed for Mummy.

'An' where your guitar?' She asked. I knew Daddy was right; he had always told me to learn to play; that a guitar was always loyal, especially if you treated it right. It was odd, but since I arrived on the island I kept remembering words of Daddy's that I now knew held wisdom. She insisted that I come into her modest home, that had two rickety chairs, a table with table-mats that had been sent from abroad. I sensed the presence of absent children. I knew that this was where Daddy had lived as a boy; that he had sat out on the veranda, looking out into the sunset, dreaming of work and dollars, and life in the big city. At that moment I felt the urge to write Daddy and tell him that I forgave him, that I understood both his anger and love, and why he kept all his feelings so private . . . She offered me food, but I refused it;

27

my thoughts were thousands of miles away, wanting to care for an old man's arthritis. She told me how her husband had worked for many years in a chemical factory in Huddersfield, how he had sent money back to her to keep her and the grandchildren and many relatives as well. Apparently, on his return, he spent one happy year in Carriacou before developing a respiratory disease and dying on the day of their wedding anniversary. Her story made me think of Daddy's fate, so I left hurriedly, but not before she had told me where my grandfather's grave was, and that I was now on Daddy's land; land he kept telling me I would one day inherit.

By this time I was emotional and weak, but I continued walking in the direction that her crooked finger had pointed. At long last I came to the grave, where an old stone stood; placed there by my father and uncles. I was now shamefully crying. Quickly I unscrewed the tops of the two bottles containing the rum and water, but as I was about to pour a little rum over the grave, an old man held up by his loyal walking stick called over to me. His smile gave his old face youth.

'Bwoy, me mout' dry; pour some in here na?' He pointed to his mouth. I was angry because he had witnessed my tears, and had stopped me at this, the most important part of my pilgrimage. He walked shakily over to me, took the bottle of rum and drank it back in just a few swigs, before smacking his lips together as Daddy always did.

'Bwoy, next time your foot reach 'pon dis spot, bring some good rum for your granddaddy.' Immediately I wanted to know how he knew that I was the grandson. As I was about to ask him, he looked down bitterly at the grave and spoke again: 'Tell him from me; a man can only inherit love; everyt'ing else jus' crumble.' With that he walked away, ignoring my jumbled questions.

When I returned to England I told Daddy the story. I remember how he froze, asking me to describe the old man. I did, recalling every detail that I could remember. There was a long silence when I finished, except for the sound of singing birds outside. Then, I suddenly realised that Daddy was crying, but I couldn't understand why. I begged him to tell me, but he seemed to rant and rave to some spirit that I too sensed was in the room. Finally he managed to throw together a few words that I could understand, taking my hand as he spoke, for the first time wanting me to know what was going on inside him.

'That old man you meet; it was your granddaddy; my father.' I now began to weep. I knew that the old man wasn't the spirit of his father, but why should I tell him otherwise, spoil the one moment that we shared together. In days to come I felt angry, for I knew that Daddy had tried, but what had the world given him: dreams and ambitions that he had striven for. And now, I was the same. Would I take the same Bible to name my newly-born son? Would my whole life be a painful adventure to try and conquer and achieve while always burdened by manhood's quest?

GLACIER MEN

JOHN FOWLES

The first trees I knew well were the apples and pears in the garden of my childhood home. This may sound rural and bucolic, but it was not, for the house was a semi-detached in a 1920s suburb at the mouth of the Thames, some forty miles from London. The back garden was tiny, less than a tenth of an acre, but my father had crammed one end and a side-fence with grid-iron espaliers and cordons. Even the minute lawn had five orchard apple trees, kept manageable only by constant debranching and pruning. It was an anomaly among our neighbours' more conventional patches, even a touch absurd, as if it were trying to be a fragment of the kitchen-garden of some great country house. No one in fact thought of it as a folly, because of the fruit those trees yielded.

The names of apples and pears are rather like the names of wines – no sure guide in themselves to quality. Two labels may read the same; but the two trees that wear them may yield fruit as different as a middling and a great vineyard from the same slope. Even the same tree can vary from year to year. As with the vine, the essential things are soil, situation, annual climate; but after those chance factors, human care. My father's trees, already happy in the alluvial clay of the area, must have been among the most closely pruned, cosseted and prayed for in the whole of England, and regularly won him prizes at local shows. They were certainly the finest-flavoured of their varieties – many increasingly rare, these supermarket days, because of their commercial disadvantages, such as tender flesh or the mysterious need to be 'eaten from the tree' – that I have ever tasted. Memories of them, of their names and flavours, Charles Ross and Lady Sudeley,

33

Peasgood's Nonsuch and King of the Pippins, haunt me still. Even the more popular kinds he grew, such as the Comice, or the Mozart and Beethoven of English pomology, James Grieve and Cox's Orange, acquired on his cunningly stunted trees a richness and subtlety I have rarely met since. This may have been partly because he knew exactly when they should be eaten. A Comice pear may take many weeks to ripen in store, but it is at its peak for only a day. Perfection in the Grieve is almost as transient.

These trees had a far greater influence on our lives than I ever realised when I was young. I took them as my father presented them to the world, as merely his hobby; as unexceptional, or inevitable, as his constant financial worries, his disappearing every day to London, his duodenal ulcer – or on a happier side his week-end golf, his tennis, his fondness for watching country cricket. But they were already more than trees, their names and habits and characters on an emotional parity with those of family.

There was already one clear difference between my father and myself, but the child I was did not recognise it, or saw it only as a matter of taste, perhaps of age, mere choice of hobby again. The difference was in any case encouraged and in my eyes sanctified by various relatives. I had an uncle who was a keen entomologist and who took me on occasional expeditions into the country – netting, sugaring, caterpillar-hunting and all the rest of it – and taught me the delicate art of 'setting' what we caught. Then there were two cousins, much older than I was. The first was a tea planter in Kenya, a keen fly fisherman and big game shot, and indisputably to me, on his occasional home leaves and visits to us, the luckiest man in the world. The other was that indispensable member of any decent middle-class English family, a determined eccentric, who no more fitted suburbia and its values than a hedgehog fits a settee. He managed to combine a bewildering set of private interests: in vintage claret, in long-distance running (where he was of international standard), in topography, and in ants, on which he was an authority. I envied him enormously his freedom to go on walking tours, his endless photography of exotic places, his sound general field knowledge of nature, and it puzzled me that my father regarded this fascinating human being as half-mad.

What these relatives very soon aroused in me was a passion for natural history and the countryside; that is, a longing to escape from those highly unnatural trees in our back garden, and all they stood for. In this, without realising it, I was already trampling over my father's soul. More and more I secretly craved everything our own environment did not possess: space, wildness, hills, woods . . . I think especially woodland, 'real' trees. With one or two exceptions – the Essex marshlands, Arctic tundra – I have always loathed flat and treeless country. Time there seems to dominate, it ticks remorselessly like a clock. But trees warp time, or rather create a variety of times: here dense and abrupt, there calm and sinuous – never plodding, mechanical, inescapably monotonous. I still feel this as soon as I enter one of the countless secret little woods in the Devon-Dorset border country where I now live; it is almost like leaving land to go into water, another medium, another dimension. When I was younger, this sensation was acute. Slinking into trees was always slinking into heaven.

Whether this rift would ever have developed as it did between my father and myself if Hitler had not been born, I cannot imagine. As it was, the hazards of the Second World War made it inevitable. We had to leave our Essex suburb for a remote Devonshire village, where all my secret yearnings were to be indulged beyond my wildest dreams. I happily forgot his little collection of crimped and cramped fruit trees in my own new world, my America of endless natural ones in Devon. I must try to convey what I now suspect his trees meant to him. As I grow older

I see that the outwardly profound difference in our attitudes to nature – especially in the form of the tree – had a strange identity of purpose, a kind of joint root-system, an interlacing, a paradoxical pattern.

My father was one of the generation whose lives were determined once and for all by the 1914–1918 War. In most outward ways he was conventional and acutely careful not to offend the mores of the two worlds he lived in, suburbia and business London. Before the war he had trained to be a solicitor; but the death of a brother at Ypres, then of his own typically late-Victorian father, twice married and leaving endless children to support, forced him into the tobacco trade. The family firm was nothing very grand. It specialised in Havana cigars, hand-made briar pipes, its own line of pure Virginia cigarettes (another lost flavour), and had two or three shops, including one in Piccadilly Arcade with a distinguished occasional clientèle. For various reasons – certainly not for lack of worrying on my father's part – it went into decline all through the 1930s, and the Second World War killed it for good. But every day when I was small my father, like most of his male neighbours, went off in suit and bowler to London: an hour by train there, an hour back. I very early decided that London was synonymous with physical exhaustion and nervous anxiety, and that the one thing I would never be was a commuter – a determination, I suspect, my father also held on my behalf, though for rather different reasons.

I can see now that the Great War took a doubly cruel toll on him – not only in those abominable years in the trenches, but in its social effect. He was given a taste of the life of the officer and gentleman, especially in the post-war period when he was in the occupation army in Germany. From then on he was condemned to the ethos and aspirations of a class, or way of life, that his increasingly unsuccessful business did not permit; and which our actual family background made rather absurd. My great-grandfather was clerk to an attorney in Somerset, and I think his father was a blacksmith. I like having such very ordinary ancestors, but my father, being only a generation away from the rise out of immemorial West Country obscurity into well-to-do mercantile London, did not. He was not a snob, he simply hankered after a grander sort of life than life allowed. (He did not even have the snob's outlet of doing something about it, since he was intensely cautious – and had to be – over money; a trait he neither inherited from his own father nor passed on to me.) It was far less that he believed in what we would call today upward social mobility than that he permanently missed the jolly expansiveness, the three-men-in-a-boatishness, of a large 1890s and Edwardian household and the style and dash of an Honourable Artillery Company mess. None of this makes him in any way unusual; but he had other private anomalies beside his little sacred grove of fruit trees.

The strangest was his fascination with philosophy. That formed three-qarters of his reading, mostly in the great Germans and the American pragmatists; the other quarter was poetry, but again almost all of it was German and French Romantic verse, very rarely English. He must have known many poems of Mörike, Droste-Hülshoff, the early Goethe, almost by heart; though he had one or two favourites such as Voltaire and Daudet, the reading in French was mainly for my sake, after it had become my 'main' subject at school and at Oxford.

He virtually never read fiction; but there was a secret. It was not until I became a novelist myself that it was disclosed. My first book was well received, film rights were sold; and suddenly one day he announced to me that he had himself long ago written a novel about his war experiences, thought that it too would 'make a good film', and asked me to read it. It was hopelessly stiff and old-fashioned, and I knew no publisher would consider it for a minute. Some of the detail of the reality of going 'over the top' in Flanders was authentic enough; and the central theme, a tale of an Englishman and his German friend in love with the same girl before the war, their coming face to face in no-man's land, death and reconciliation there, was like all baldly summarised novel themes, intrinsically neither good nor bad. But it read as if it were by someone (as it indeed was) who had read hardly a single word of all the other English fiction and poetry the Great War had produced: no Owen, no Rosenberg, no Sassoon, no Graves, no Manning . . . it was so innocent of all their sophistication, technically and emotionally, that it almost had a curiosity value, as a period piece. I asked him if he would like me to see about getting it privately printed, but he wanted his son's sort of good fortune, public acceptance and success, and I had to tell him the cruel truth.

I am sure the greatest shock for him, when I first told him I was to be published, had been the financial side; for the anomalous counterpart to this anomalous love of philosophy and Romantic verse was an obsession with yield. Just as he endlessly tended his fruit trees, so did he endlessly tend his stocks and shares in the *Financial Times* – I think probably with equal skill, though he never had very much to invest. Indeed the two things became somehow intertwined, for part of the fruit-harvesting ritual every autumn was the calculation of how much the fruit would have fetched *if* it had been sold to some local greengrocer; in fact the always considerable surplus was handed out to relations and neighbours, but I am sure this hypothetical 'dividend' was important to him. The highest praise he ever bestowed on his own produce was to say how much it had been publicly fetching the week before, as if that somehow added a cachet which superb flavour and condition could never grant. It was not the somewhat scandalous – in suburban terms – content of *The Collector* that worried him nearly so much as the thought that it might be a failure; and then, when that hurdle was overcome, that I might leave the sound, if humble, economic safety-net of teaching for full-time writing. In his eyes that was like selling a blue chip for a flagrant gamble.

All I could eventually do about his own novel was to use some fragments of battlefield description in a passage of *The Magus*. But just before he died I was sitting one afternoon by his bedside in a hospital; he was in pain and drugged, and seemingly asleep. Then suddenly he began to talk, a strange rattle of staccato sentences, a silence, then more, another silence. It was to do with some friend being killed beside him during an attack, and was told in terms of a dialogue between my father and a third person who had also been there. It was not in the least said for me, but came out of his near coma. There was no time, it was now again, and eternally now; infinitely more vivid in those snatches of broken sentence than in anything he had written – or indeed ever told me – of his battlefield experiences in his more conscious moments. They had always been taboo. Memories of Ypres and other shattered towns, château billets out of the line, life in occupied Cologne, yes; but never the core of it, to those who have not known it: the running, walking, plodding through wire and craters into any moment's death.

Beside his bed that day I thought of all the crossroads in our two lives where I had murdered him, or at least what he believed in, and in particular of one of his major life-decisions, never forgiven on my part, though I had long ceased to suffer from it. This went back to the end of the Second World War.

We had spent that, self-evacuated, in a cottage of the Devonshire village I fictionalised in *Daniel Martin*. Despite the external horrors and deprivations of the time, they were for me

39

JOHN FOWLES

fertile and green-golden years. I learnt nature for the first time in a true countryside among true countrymen, and from then on I was irredeemably lost as a townsman. I have had to spend long years in cities since then, but never willingly, always in daily exile. I even preferred the antiquated class-system of village life, with its gentry and its 'peasants' and infinite grades between, to the uniformity of street after suburban street of same houses, same fears, same pretensions. But then, once the war was over, my father decided that we must quit the green paradise and return to the grey limbo. Neither of his overt reasons – business and the need to be near London – seemed to me honest. The family firm was virtually wound up, he had no cultural interests (unless one counts professional cricket) that were deprived by the distance of London from Devon.

I can guess now that the experience of village social distinctions, that ancient nose for the difference between status gained by money or education and status grown from ancestry, or generations of 'breeding', had upset him. But I think it was above all the breadth of choice, in terms of how and where you live, that he really disliked in the country. Some of the larger houses and gardens in our village must have corresponded to his dream; but they did not necessarily give status there. The place's most obvious gentleman (another murder at the crossroads, since he took me under his wing and taught me to fish and shoot – and poach) lived in one of its smallest cottages.

I sense that the memory of suburbia must have represented to my father (in what was also a completely new experience for him) something like the famous old fellowship of the trenches, the consoling feeling of everyone being in the same boat; all genteelly in the same reduced financial circumstances, with the same vague hopes, abiding by the same discreetly agreed codes. Things were far too transparent in Devon, too close to unfair value-systems that were in turn too close to nature; and towards nature my father showed not only no interest, but a distinct hostility (generally muted, before my own passion, into a kind of sceptical incredulity). He would claim he had seen enough open country and breathed enough open air in his three years in Flanders to last him his lifetime; and he regarded even the shortest walks, the simplest picnics away from houses and roads as incipiently dangerous, so many steps towards total anarchy. The only exception was golf, but I think that even there he regarded the rough and the surrounding woods – on the course he played – as something more than just a game hazard. The last country walk I recall attempting with him was in the Essex marshlands. He walked two or three hundred yards from where we had parked along a sea wall, then refused point-blank to go any further against a lifetime's instincts. He was old then, but quite happy still to walk two or three miles on town pavements.

He had in fact a number of the traits, both good and bad, of what used to be called the ghetto mentality: on the one hand, a keen admiration of intellectual achievement and of financial acumen (skill with yield), a love of the emotional, the Mendelssohnian, in things like poetry and classical music, of brilliant virtuoso performances (he had no time for garden plants that did not put on 'a good show'), of quintessentially city arts like the music-hall (though one of his sisters who had had the temerity to enter that last world, and once understudied Gertie Millar, was cast eternally beyond the pale); on the other, an almost total blindness to nature. This 'Jewishness' was not totally unconscious in him. Suburban neighbours who showed a stock anti-semitism usually received very short shrift; a bludgeoning of Spinoza, perhaps, or Heine, or Einstein, and then a general lecture on what European intellectual and artistic history owed to Jewish genius. He had been a military prosecutor in Cologne, and seen most of the great Edwardian counsels in action before the war, and knew how to browbeat the shifty witness. Philosophical arguments with him could grow painfully like cross-examination, far more forensic than Socratic, and I have shunned the logical ever since.

Children are notoriously blind towards their parents, and nowhere more than in failing to see the childlike in them – the inescapable conditioning of the past. In the beginning we all try to attribute to our parents what used to be attributed to God: limitless power to intervene, indisputable wisdom. The theological concept was clearly no more than an idealisation of this. Its flaw is the inevitable confusion between authority and free will – the jointly held delusion that possessing one must entail possessing the other. I am sure in retrospect that the decision to return to suburbia was well beyond my father's free will; he could not *not* do it, any more than he could prevent that terrible memory from the Great War bubbling to the surface when he lay on his deathbed. But I did at that moment guess what had truly inspired the retreat from Devon.

It was not financial caution or love of suburbia in itself, it was not anything but his trees and the sanctuary they offered ... in no sense, in that minute garden, a physical sanctuary, but a kind of poetic one, however banal the surroundings: a place he could control, that was different from all around it, not least in its huge annual yield of fruit. It stood in effect as the very antithesis of a battlefield, including the metaphorical one of wild nature; and of course it could not be reproduced anywhere else, since he had personally created and cherished it. We lived in Devon surrounded by farm orchards, but what he needed was the fruits of his own cultivation, the knowledge he had gained of every habit, every whim, every fruiting spur (all infertile shoots were ruthlessly extirpated) of each of his score of trees. He had himself been severely pruned by history and family circumstance, and this was his answer, his reconciliation to his fate – his Platonic ideal of the strictly controlled and safe, his Garden of Eden. All my adolescent and older loathing of its social and physical environment – and my mother was on my side – can have only deepened his attachment.

Those trees were in fact his truest philosophy, and his love of actual philosophy, the world of abstract ideas, was essentially (like his love of trenchant lawyers, with secateurs in their mouths) no more than a facet of his hatred of natural disorder. Good philosophers prune the chaos of reality and train it into fixed shapes, thereby forcing it to yield valuable and delicious fruit – or at least in theory. One of my father's heroes was Bertrand Russell, for whose incisive intellect and more popular philosophical works he had the greatest admiration; yet he had the very reverse for Russell's later political attitudes. It was almost as if he had let one of his cordons grow as it liked, a blasphemous breaking of his own eleventh commandment: Thou shalt prune all trees.

I had always seen this as the great difference between us; and puzzling, genetically mysterious. What he abhorred, I adored. My own 'orchards' were, from the moments I first knew them, the forgotten and increasingly deserted copses and woods of the West of England, and later, of France. I still grow some of my father's favourite apples, such as James Grieve, and some of my own, such as D'Arcy Spice, but I won't use sprays and don't prune properly – with no excuse, since he taught me the rudiments of that art. Yet I see now that our very different attitudes to these things were really the same phenomenon, the same tree. His refusal to be moved by what moved me in nature was perhaps largely a product of his own conditioning; but its function (without my realising it, of course) was very similar to what pruning does for young fruit trees – that is, to direct their growth and determine their future.

43

Successful artistic parents seem very rarely to give birth to equally successful artistic sons and daughters, and I suspect it may be because the urge to create, which must always be partly the need to escape everyday reality, is better fostered – despite modern educational theory – not by a sympathetic and 'creative' childhood environment, but the very opposite, by pruning and confining natural instinct. (Nine-tenths of all artistic creation derives its basic energy from the engine of repression and sublimation, and well beyond the strict Freudian definition of those terms.) That I should have differed so much from my father in this seems to me in retrospect not in the least a matter for Oedipal guilt, but a healthy natural process, just as the branches of a healthy tree do not try to occupy one another's territory. That they grow in different directions and ways does not mean that they do not share a same mechanism of need, a same set of deeper rules.

I think I truly horrified him only once in my life, which was when, soon after coming into possession, I first took him around my present exceedingly unkempt, unmanaged and unmanageable garden. I had previously shocked him by buying a derelict farm; but its thirty acres of scrub and rough pasture were sanity (at least I let the keep and got some token yield from it) beside this new revelation of folly. He thought it madness to take on such a 'jungle', and did not believe me when I said I saw no need to take it on, only to leave it largely alone, in effect to my co-tenants, its wild birds and beasts, its plants and insects. He would never have conceded that it was my equivalent of his own beautifully disciplined apples and pears, and just as much cultivated, though not in a literal sense. He would not have understood that something I saw down there just an hour ago, at this moment I write – two tawny owlets fresh out of the nest, sitting on a sycamore branch like a pair of badly knitted Christmas stockings and ogling down at this intruder into *their* garden – means to me exactly what the Horticultural Society cups on his sideboard used to mean to him: a token of order in unjust chaos, the reward of perseverance in a right philosophy. That his chaos happens to be my order is not, I think, very important.

He sent me two cordon pear trees to plant, soon after that first visit. They must be nearly fifteen years old now; and every year, my soil being far too thin and dry for their liking, they produce a few miserable fruit, or more often none at all. I would never have them out. It touches me that they should so completely take his side; and reminds me that practically everyone else in my life – even friends who profess to be naturalists – has also taken his side; that above all the world in general continues to take his side. No fruit for those who do not prune; no fruit for those who question knowledge; no fruit for those who hide in trees untouched by man; no fruit for traitors to the human cause.

All you have read so far comes from a text I wrote in the 1970s, *The Tree*. What I can now belatedly see in the 1990s is that I never really knew my father, or rather, our relationship; or more precisely still, sensed the distances and silences between us. It is easy enough to recognise similar traits of taste and character, even some psychological weaknesses and twists, but far more difficult to distinguish nature's cleverest trick: letting children grow so far, so bewilderingly different, from their parents. The breaks in the line, the gaps, the lacunae, seem almost a kind of divine carelessness, a dismissive snub of the supposedly infallible genetic code. I optimistically likened us in *The Tree* to 'wise' branches; a better comparison would have been with machines, set like locomotives on fixed tracks. We had such cramped perspectives, there were such appalling blinkers on how we behaved and thought.

I realise now that he severely pruned me by telling me so little of himself, in part obeying his own intense hatred of any exposure and over-intimacy. This may be attributed in turn to his own boyhood experiences of a large family, and to the far grimmer ones of the 1914–1918 War, but the true blame for this largely unconscious process of glaciation, this effort to create chill distances, seems very clearly to me to lie with the historical situation into which we were both born. I now deeply lament (not curse, that is pointless) the stiff, almost Prussian, middle-class culture and code, the caste system, in which we were both brought up. I can see now that it very seriously warped his life, and I'm far from sure whether it has not distorted mine in many ways I don't like to have to admit. One has certainly been a lifelong political unease – failing to be a decent socialist, yet being even less able to make a decent (if there is such a thing) conservative. No political party has ever really suited me; and I suspect it was always the same for my father. Both of us wanted to fit, in our very different ways; and somehow never did. So much of both our lives has had to be devoted to queasily pretending and reluctantly conforming.

The standards by which we were forced to judge and value other men and women now seem ludicrously antiquated. Only last week I chanced to read a history of the Hittites, of the second and third millenia before Christ. What surprised me was not how remote they seemed, but how close; how incomprehensibly little humanity had progressed – especially in psychological and emotional matters – in the last three thousand years. Why did my father and I so very rarely touch, let alone embrace? Why did not only he, but I also, always maintain the age-gap between us as if it were some form of clothing that would leave us naked if we omitted it? Why am I so remote from him? Past history seems full of examples of filial reverence and piety, why do I not feel it? Why do I hardly ever think of him these days? It perhaps seems obvious that I always surreptitiously disliked, even detested him.

Yet I am quite certain I did not. I have absolutely no belief in any afterlife. I greatly admired, only this last year, the geologist Stephen Jay Gould's sobering recent book, *Wonderful Life*, with its ruthless dowsing of so much of the rather fatuous self-esteem of the human species. Over twenty years ago I wrote a poem about my father, which, very typically, I never dared show him. Both our sadness and our mystery lay less in what I did not say (I loved him) than that I could not. That great cultural glacier, which I think of now as the last and perhaps most fatal bequest of the British Empire, froze so many others besides us, and not only in the middle classes. I hope a thaw has now begun, and pray the future will not too contemptuously mock our choked, self-murdered spirits.

In Chalkwell Park

the staring-green October green
the common grass intent on thriving
out of step
when all else dies this is the season

we walk
this tired municipal park
and Sunday sky
we walk the grass
my slow father and I

and the sun is tepidly warm
the sky a non-committal blue
with a few clouds dying
the death of leaves
mourning chrysanthemums
Li Po
we inspect the Michaelmas daisies
a new dwarf stock
a milky blue

and death

I cannot say
swift passage
I cannot say

most natural thing
and cannot say
cannot say

he mumbles on
'I thought it would be fine,
the glass was high'

cannot say
do not die
my father my father do not die

1961

SCENES FROM SON-HOOD

DAVID EPSTEIN

The University of Berlin, 1934, ten years before my birth. He has come from Pennsylvania, the son of Russian immigrants, to do graduate work in German literature. Registration takes place in a large hall, filled with students.

He gets to the head of his line, a small American flag pinned to his lapel, and the Registrar asks him a question, in German, which he has not asked anyone preceding him.

'What percentage non-Aryan are you?'

'One hundred percent American,' he says, his face flushed. The man asks again, raising his voice. 'What percentage non-Aryan are you?'

The huge room suddenly goes silent, focusing on them. He leans forward, pounds his fist on to the table, and shouts in the man's face, 'One hundred percent non-Aryan. One hundred percent American!'

The whole room bursts into applause. He is twenty-four.

How much of memory is limned with wishing? Was he the man I saw, or the man I wanted to see? Do we embroider for the dead?

My father believed in me. From boyhood, I had an inherent sense of being loved, and valued. Such good fortune, however, does not come without its burden of unspoken expectation. I knew I had to deliver. Failure has always been the dragon in the closet of my life; I have kept a foot against the door, and used synonyms.

He ran an organisation which fought bigotry and racial discrimination; dealt with Presidents and Prime Ministers,

Senators and Governors. Through educational programs and moral suasion he pressed people in power to open doors to minorities. As a child I understood that his job was different from most fathers' and I felt proud of what he did, although I had some trouble defining it. He travelled too much, however, and I missed him the way a child can miss a parent, with a palpable longing, a physical vacancy which could only be filled when he walked in the door and I had my arms around him again.

I watched him bound off to work every morning, fully engaged in the pursuit of his job. By the time I was a teenager I was convinced that, like him, whatever I was going to do with my life must be wedded to who I was, so that my whole being would be involved in my work. Anything else, I concluded, would be a fake life.

A thoughtful, patient man, my father was a safe haven in my struggle towards manhood. However buffeted, I always had his quiet confidence to depend upon. And yet it was precisely this evenness of temper, his loving acceptance, which I had to challenge. To stake out my own territory I wanted to do something exciting and daring. I developed a dreadful need to astonish the man.

He co-authored a number of books on anti-Semitism. Material was researched by assistants who followed the outlines he and his partner had drawn up. The two of them would then transcribe the data into chapters. I knew, however, that he was not truly a writer, nor did he consider himself one. At seventeen, having fallen in love with Joseph Conrad, I decided I was going to become the real thing.

He and my mother were quietly horrified. I had been raised to be a success – but a writer? They suggested a less precarious route, journalism, or the law, 'in conjunction with writing'. I shook my head. How can you start an adventure with a compromise?

A few weeks after his seventieth birthday party (I was thirty-eight), he called and told me that a tumor had been found, and an operation immediately scheduled. He had never been seriously ill. 'How do you feel about it?' I asked. He hesitated. 'Concerned,' he said.

Some question! What did I expect him to say. 'Wonderful?' 'Terrified?' It took me a little longer to get in touch with how I felt about it. Two nights later, while our daughters slept across the hall, I awakened screaming frantically, 'Don't let them hurt my Daddy!'

Parents and children often reconcile or express unspoken feelings during such crises, but my father and I had never been separated, except by minor disagreements, and there was no need to start talking about love. It was constant.

While he was in the hospital, recovering from the operation, and then at home in their apartment with my mother, we spent a great deal of time together. We talked. I often held his hand while he lay in bed, or sat in a chair. I had a tough time letting go of him. As his strength waned, I wandered through memories of our life together, growing up, and growing older.

The day after President Kennedy was shot, colleges closed down, and I came home, shaken and adrift. I wanted to be anchored near my father. We watched the news on television, and we walked together. We walked all over Manhattan those first few days. Sometimes it rained. We kept walking. We spoke very little.

He was one of life's naturally positive people. I could feel him struggling to make sense out of what had happened, looking for a path beyond disillusionment for us both. During one of our outings, we stopped on the corner of Second Avenue and Fifty-third street. He looked up at me, (I was six-foot one, he was five-eight) and he said, 'Promise me one thing. Promise me this will not make you a cynical person.' I was nineteen; I promised.

He and my mother journeyed to Connecticut to attend the first night of my first play, produced in graduate school. The theatre was a basement room beneath one of the colleges. It was L-shaped. We had built the set at the right angle, and placed the audience at both ends.

I smiled as I watched my parents descend into this theatrical cave, and apprehensively take their seats – in folding chairs. They were used to Broadway comfort, and I was about to introduce them to real theatre.

The actors ignited the play that evening, and when the lights came up the response was strong. My father stood nearby and watched, hawk-eyed, as people pounded my back and threw their arms around me.

We walked together towards a restaurant, and I glanced over at him. I saw a look of relieved amazement on his face, and sensed a sudden lightening of spirit. His and mine. In one evening I had managed to begin my career and astound my father. I was filled with a great sense of power and well-being.

One afternoon when he was in the hospital, I reminded him of a crucial phone conversation from years earlier. I was home from college, and in love with a girl who was leaving to study in England. She had her own apartment. The impending separation was making for an emotional evening, and when I looked up it was almost two a.m. My parents were expecting me. I had either to go, or to call. I wanted to stay, but sleeping over was not something I was in the habit of revealing. By now my father would be in deep shut-eye, and my mother would be reading beside him, waiting up for me. She was inescapable.

I knew she would grab the phone when it rang. If I told her I wasn't coming home, I would have had an inquisition on my hands. I decided to try what had worked most of my life; I'd let my father handle it.

'Mom, everything's alright. Let me speak to Dad, please.'

'What's the matter! Where are you?'

'Nothing's the matter. Please put Dad on the phone.'

'It's two a.m.! Where are you?'

'Put Dad on!'

Finally I hear his sleepy voice, 'Hi Ep.'

(And in the background, 'Where is he? What's going on?')

'Dad, everything's fine. I'm not coming home tonight. I'm staying here. I'm fine.'

(In the background again, 'What is going on?')

'OK, Ep,' he says calmly, 'we'll see you tomorrow.'

(And, before the phone is put down, 'Where is he? Why isn't he . . .')

Click.

Sitting across from his hospital bed, I told him it had been the most reassuring click of my young life.

The television reviews of my first commercial play in New York were negative. At the opening night party my father stood in front of a TV screen, and shouted his disagreement at one talking head after another, then left, despondent. Later in the evening, when the *New York Times* delivered a rave, he was ecstatic. Through him, I sensed that I had arisen phoenix-like from the ashes of failure, and felt heroic.

A couple of years afterwards, the same newspaper panned a play of mine. He saw the review first, and called to deliver the bad news. His voice had such a dreadful, funereal tone, my heart began to pound. He sounded as if he were announcing my death.

During the weeks he was hospitalised, I spent every morning rewriting a play at my desk, before walking to see him in the afternoon. I had focus, and worked hard, pushing away the troubling world I had to deal with later each day. The result was a Broadway option which thrilled him when I reported it, although he never got to see the play. (Neither did Broadway, but that's another story.)

I yearned for him each evening after I left his side, and walked west across Manhattan, protected by an armor of emotion. I felt if anyone came near me, threatened me, I would destroy them with rage. I could not be hurt more than I was hurting; my anger and sorrow made me invulnerable.

We didn't always connect. In the last, tumultuous months of high school I had become terrified of potential dismemberment at the hands of a girlfriend's father. Her mother had discovered our affair, and threatened me with disclosing it to her husband. 'He would come after you,' she promised, 'with an axe.'

For the remainder of the school year I sat in a defensive posture, facing the classroom door. At night I couldn't sleep, worried the doorbell might ring. I prayed.

One evening that spring my father came into my room. We chatted while I silently screamed for help. He lingered, sensing something. Finally, he asked me if everything was alright. I could almost taste the relief I would feel unburdening myself to him. I tried to let the words out, but something locked them in. I have always thought it was teenage embarrassment; sex was not something we talked about. I suspect now that I feared by admitting the nature of my terror, I would be exposed to failure in his eyes. I would be letting him down just by having gotten myself into such a situation. I remained silent. He left the room.

Part of his charm was his buoyant enthusiasm, an almost pre-Freudian, country-boy-in-the-big-city spirit. If he could have discussed sex with me, demystified it, brought it into our dialogue, perhaps he might have kept me from a good deal of anguish. Sex became a furtive, unintegrated presence, a fearful delight. It was something one did to people, rather than with them. Unfortunately, I operated on that level for many years.

Later that same spring my college admission letters were scheduled to arrive. I had aimed high in my applications. On the Saturday when they were due, I stepped out of my room to an unusual quiet. My father appeared from the kitchen. My mother was nowhere to be seen. I told him I wanted to go downstairs to check the mailbox. I started out.

'They came!' he said, before I got to the door. As I turned around I sensed an odd tremor in his usually steady voice.

'Where are they?' I asked, glancing at the table.

He came up to me.

'They're all rejections!' he said, almost shouting. And then he threw his arms around me, and cried out,

'The bastards!'

As we held on to one another I was shocked to feel him shake with emotion. His distress numbed me, and it took a few moments for my own to surface. I remember thinking, 'If he's so upset, this must be a disaster.' I was suddenly confronted with undeniable, seismographic failure.

Whom had I failed? I was much too involved with my own feelings of worthlessness to be aware of having disappointed anyone. To be seventeen and clobbered so resoundingly is the emotional equivalent of a head-on collision with a cement truck. I have always thought that my father's low-key parental approach had the opposite effect of the domineering, cartoon father making

59

demands, and that it was because of my own intense temperament that I placed great pressure upon myself. But perhaps his kind of unspoken expectation is even more powerful than the macho, overt variety; more powerful because it assumes success.

Who had opened my mail, and why my mother had vanished that morning were not hard questions for me to unravel. They only served to underline my sense of calamity. She couldn't face seeing me. My father had handled it.

The phone rang for him early one evening when he was home from the hospital. I heard him talking to someone he clearly didn't know well. Some decision was required, and he declined to make it. I heard him say, 'I'm afraid I can't tell you that. David Epstein is the head of this family now.' And he hung up.

I felt a chill. We had gotten hints that he had alluded to the gravity of his illness to his friends, but never to us. That he chose not to be open with us about it, was in character. His job had been to smooth troubled waters, to bring contentious groups together in compromise. He had done the same within the family. He was the peacemaker. It would have been unthinkable for him to force us all to openly confront something so dire.

It confirmed what I suspected. His object was to protect us, and I suppose, in the process, protect himself from seeing our despair.

His sense of humor was subtle and sharp. Around the dinner table one teenage night someone mentioned shopping at the local boutiques. My mother, a big woman, said she couldn't stand those shops. She began to carry on about the snobbishness of the salespeople, the outrageous prices they charged, the claustrophobia of the dressing rooms. In the middle of it, my father turned to me and said quietly, 'She's afraid they won't carry her size.'

I began to laugh. I laughed so hard I slid off my chair and rolled on the dining-room floor. Across the table, insulted, my mother fumed.

'Get up! Get up, Ep!' He pleaded, bending over me, laughing, and in big trouble. 'Get off the floor!'

In the early seventies I was asked by his colleagues to write a presentation for their organization's annual meeting. He was very pleased when I accepted the offer. It was during the Vietnam war, and I couldn't restrain myself from injecting a little anti-war sentiment into the material. It was not entirely irrelevant to the evening, but for an organization which was supposed to be apolitical, it was critical of the Nixon White House.

The men I was working with wanted it removed, but I wouldn't do it. I told my father I was having a problem with them, and he said, not unexpectedly, 'Let me handle them.' Apparently he said the same thing to them about me, because on the evening of the black-tie affair at the Waldorf Astoria he read his portion of the script to the well-heeled audience, and eliminated all references to the war.

I was apoplectic. When he congratulated me on how well it went, I accused him of selling out. He dismissed my tirade as 'nonsense'. I turned away from him, and left the hotel. He had obviously made the decision that it would be less problematical to offend me, than the U.S. government. It was the only time I can remember feeling as if he had let me down. We never spoke of it again.

One afternoon I wheeled my father to the basement of the hospital to get his blast of radiation. He had managed to maintain his good spirits, convinced or trying to convince us, that he was going to beat this disease.

We talked politics on our way to the elevator and on the ride down. Once we got into the basement we had to wait our turn. I looked around and cringed. Without exception the people surrounding us were dreadfully ill, missing hair, limbs, and any appearance of strength. I fought a sudden urge to turn him around, and rush back upstairs to the privacy of his room so that he wouldn't see what was so obvious to me. I wanted to protect his optimism, to keep him buoyant so that I might remain afloat. I was afraid that his loss of spirit would devastate me.

He took a deep breath, and wheeled himself in for his appointment.

When my sister and I were children, he seemed to be on a mission to describe his father, who died while he was in college. Through him, my grandfather's image became indelible.

Before he emigrated to America, my grandfather was conscripted into the Russian army. He had the wit to join the orchestra because it was the best fed unit in a time when many starved. He faked playing the clarinet until fellow band-members instructed him. I asked why he had chosen the clarinet? My father laughed, and said it was because it was light, and easy to carry.

There was an heroic, hard-working sternness about my grandfather, leavened by a bitingly acute sense of humor. He and my grandmother settled in a small Pennsylvania city, and became proprietors of a general store, across from a steel mill. They awakened at four-thirty every morning, closed up at eight every night.

The first play I wrote for public television was set in my grandparents' store. (My father hung posters in his office, and had cards printed up announcing its air-time.)

The store still exists. The property has long since passed into other hands. Across the street is the row-house in which my father grew up. The steel-mill still hums. It's a black neighborhood now.

I stepped inside the store. It had been twenty years since my last visit. It was now a fast-food restaurant, fried chicken, fried onion rings, barbecued ribs. There were a few formica tables and chairs, but mostly it appeared to be a take-out spot.

I looked around, trying to picture it as it had been when my father was a boy. I bought a pack of lifesavers, and asked the woman at the register if she was the owner? She pointed towards a man further along the counter, cutting up pieces of chicken.

I introduced myself to a black man who had a Jamaican accent. I told him that my grandfather had owned the store sixty years ago. He wanted to know the family name and what the store had been like. We chatted a while.

Here was another immigrant using the same building my grandfather had used to dig his roots in America, trying to make his family's mark.

My mother was waiting for me in the Mercedes-Benz my father had bought her, and we drove away. When I arrived home I gave my children a present from their great-grandfather's store. Lifesavers.

He had some difficulty buying that car. When he was nearing retirement, he called me one afternoon, and said they had been out auto shopping. I asked what they had looked at, and he said a Dodge, a Plymouth, a Chevrolet. I said I didn't understand why he was considering cars that were bound to fall apart after a couple of years.

'What do you suggest,' he said.

'What's the nicest car you've ever driven?'

'Well,' he hesitated a moment, 'we once rented a Mercedes-Benz when we were in Europe. That was some car, but . . .'

'So get a Mercedes.'

'Don't be ridiculous!'

'What's ridiculous about getting what you want? You'll probably never have to buy yourself another car, if you get a Mercedes.'

'I couldn't do it,' he said.

'Why not?' I asked.

'What would people think?'

'Dad,' I said, 'you're a successful man, what do you give a shit what people think?'

He laughed a surprised, child-like laugh.

On the day he got it, he took me for a ride in a dark blue 240D, and enumerated all the reasons why it was the best car made. He had forgotten our conversation.

I am constantly tuning in my father, scrambling to bring him into touch with my children. I want to give them as much detail as I possibly can, so they can paint a picture of him to hang in their own imaginations, as I did with my grandfather. Will that need dissipate ten years from now? Will I have succeeded?

My mother called me in for dinner. The past few days my father had been struggling just to get out of bed. He looked up from his pillow and said he wanted to join us. At the door, my mother questioned the wisdom of such an attempt. He responded by saying, 'Help me up, Ep.'

He had lost his strength. I helped him stand, positioned myself behind him, locked my arms under his armpits, supporting him, and we stepped around the bed, in tight tandem. Half way across the room, he stopped and rested against his bureau, out of breath. When we started out again, my mother, in tears at the door, said, 'No. Take him back, he can't make it!'

Suddenly, I felt his entire body surge with strength. 'Who can't make it?' he said, shrugging me off. He proceeded to walk straight into the dining-room, where he took his seat at the head of the table. It was his last meal out of bed.

Fishing was his great escape. When I was a boy he and a group of other fathers arranged expeditions by hired jeep, travelling eight miles along the beach to the end of our vacation island, where the surfcasting was famous.

He would set his alarm for four in the morning, tip-toe into the kitchen, make sandwiches and a thermos of coffee, put hot chocolate up for me, and then climb the stairs, and awaken me with a kiss.

I'd jump out of bed, pull on my cold jeans, and join him at the kitchen table for a cup of steaming, milky-sweet cocoa. Then the two of us would gather our fishing gear, walk in the dark to the beach, where we'd meet the other fathers and sons, and await the headlights of the open truck coming towards us along the water's edge.

As the driver followed the rutted tracks left by previous beach buggies, we would huddle together against the morning chill, and watch the sun rise over the lead-gray Atlantic. It was the magic hour, when the fish were said to be at their most engaging.

The beach expeditions phased out as my father gradually shifted his energies from the surf to an outboard motorboat he abused on the Great South Bay.

Although most of his vacation time and weekends were spent on the water, he never mastered the techniques of boating. Perhaps to compensate, he bought himself every gadget on the market, from a depth-finder, which was supposed to help locate schools of fish, but didn't, to a CB radio, installed to keep him in touch with land, which, since he tended to hug the shore, was never more than fifty yards away.

He had a remarkably unselfconscious nature. If a problem arose he would simply reach out for assistance. Anybody within hailing distance was a potential savior. As a teenager I found this mortifying. Even as a grown man I would cringe when he proudly told me how had 'solved' a boating problem.

On a beautiful summer afternoon he returned from an adventure, showering praise on the U.S. Coast Guard. He couldn't say enough about them.

'These were wonderful boys, Ep. Real gentlemen.'

'What happened, Dad?' I asked, holding my breath.

'My battery conked out, or the starter-motor – maybe it was the gas-line. But thank God for that CB!'

I paused. 'You radioed the Coast Guard?'

'It worked beautifully. They asked my exact location, and told me not to worry, they'd have a boat there in twenty minutes.'

'What *was* your location, Dad?'

'In the channel, right out in front of our marina. They were there in nineteen minutes on the nose.'

'Dad, you were forty feet from shore! There must have been a hundred boats around you.'

'Not everybody has a CB.'

'You could've waved, you could've *paddled* in!'

'Ep, this is their *job*.'

He began to experience back pains before the cancer was diagnosed, and tried various stretching exercises to ease the discomfort. One evening when he was hurting, I volunteered to massage him. He took off his shirt and stretched out. I went to work.

As I pushed into his lower back, the sudden, jellied shifting of his flesh beneath my fingertips startled me. I was repulsed, and almost pulled my hands away. My experience had been exclusively with youthful bodies, but my father's flesh was no longer close to the bone. It felt loose and strangely treacherous, as if I might push him right out of his skeleton.

I kept moving my hands up and down alongside his spine, and he told me how good it felt. Gradually I relaxed, and began to enjoy the fact that I was helping him.

What I discovered that afternoon was the physical aspect of his aging. I had touched his mortality, and it had terrified me. Yet the contact also brought us closer together, and perhaps, unconsciously prepared me for what was to happen a year or so later.

As much as he loved to fish, I couldn't bear it. To be alone with him, however, I frequently joined the hunt. He was not the calm, assured man on water that he was on land. While I was looking for a few hours of peace and relaxation in his company, Dad was restlessly scouting blue-fish. We would reach one of his favorite 'spots', where his hook had been ingested by fish past, take a few unsuccessful casts, and while I was enjoying the sun and the breeze, he would be ready to move on.

During one expedition I actually hooked a big one. I knew it was big because we could see it approaching the boat as I reeled in my line. Dad was thrilled. He shouted encouragement and instruction at the same time. 'Look at that sonofabitch, Ep! You got him! Easy, easy! don't yank him, grab the net, scoop him up, scoop him into . . .' The fish spit the hook.

Dad snatched the net from me, and practically dove in after the disappearing tail fin, yelling in dismay, 'You lost him! Goddamit, you lost him!'

I had rarely seen him so animated. I was calm, which only agitated him more.

'You should've gotten the net *under* him,' he said, glaring at me.

'Right, I should've,' I said.

He shook his head. I shrugged, noticing the stunning sunset over his shoulder. We were looking for different things.

One summer morning, long before our children arrived, my wife and I accepted an invitation to visit a friend a few miles down the beach. My father knew the woman too, and we asked him to join us. We brought our golden retriever, and met him at the marina.

It was a sunny, windy day. The bay was chopped with white-caps. My father took one look, suggested we forgo the boat, and walk the three miles down the beach. I managed to convince him that the danger was minimal, and we boarded.

The ride took only a few minutes. When we got to our friend's little village we had to moor the boat some yards out, and wade ashore. She was at the water's edge, waving to us. The dog leaped in and paddled around as we slipped over the side of the boat. Dad was concerned about getting his pants wet, so he took them off.

One of the lasting images I have of him is with his jeans held above his head, emerging triumphantly from Great South Bay to hug our friend, wearing his jockey shorts; not unlike MacArthur, re-taking the Philippines.

When we returned to the boat late that afternoon, the tide had risen. The water was chest high on me, and almost up to my father's neck. I gave my wife a hand scrambling in, and we both managed to hoist the dog aboard. I couldn't boost my father up, and he couldn't pull himself in. He was uncertain in the water, and no longer agile enough to do it alone.

I finally decided to deposit him in the boat. I lifted him under the knees and behind his shoulders, and raised him to the surface. I had the odd sensation of cradling a child. When he said, very sternly, 'Don't drop me, Ep,' the contrast between his infantile position in my arms, and the parental tone of his voice, struck me as very funny. I strained to raise him over the gunnels, started laughing, and practically dumped him into the boat, where my grinning wife and barking dog cushioned his delivery.

For short periods during his hospital stay the chemicals being pumped into his body affected my father's mind. His voice was strong and confident, but what he said was not always logical. People would call him, and he'd have conversations which occasionally left them perplexed. It was a delicate time because we wanted to treat him with the respect he commanded, but we also wanted to protect him from the difficulties such conversations might produce.

One afternoon my mother and I were in the room with him, reading quietly. He looked up and said, 'Ep, get me Tony S. (a business associate) on the phone.'

My mother blanched, and said, 'You just spoke to him, Ben.'

'Well, I need to speak to him again. Dial him for me, Ep.'

'OK, Dad,' I said, not moving, 'let me finish what I'm reading.'

His just-completed conversation with this fellow, a busy lawyer, had been slightly off the mark, and I had no intention of placing the call for him, but I needed to play for time.

When my mother heard me agree to make the call, however, she stood up, and fearing that he would embarrass himself, repeated the fact that he had just spoken to the man, and stormed out of the room, furious at me.

I kept reading the paper, desperately hoping he would forget about the request. He asked again. Again I put him off, telling him I was almost finished with my article. What could I say that wouldn't upset or humiliate him? I wasn't going to tell him that he was not thinking rationally, or that he would annoy the man by calling again. I couldn't pretend the fellow's line was busy or that he was out; he might call him on his own when I was out of the room. All these things flashed through my mind, until he finally complained and urged me to make the call.

I put the paper down slowly, and got to my feet, still not knowing what I was about to do. I walked towards the night-table, and as I reached for the phone I had what was perhaps the most intuitive moment of our relationship.

'Dad, why don't you let me handle Tony S.?' I said, surprising myself. I knew nothing about what he and this man ordinarily discussed. If my father were suddenly cogent, he'd consider my offer inane and condescending.

He looked up. A flash of recognition seemed to pass across his eyes. '*You* want to handle Tony S.?'

'Yes,' I said, 'why don't you leave it to me. I'll get in touch with him.'

He considered a moment. I watched his body relax against the pillows. 'That's a good idea,' he said, nodding. He closed his eyes, and napped. Tony S. was never mentioned again.

I was elated that I had avoided a tight situation by coming up with the catch-phrase he had used at difficult times in my life, 'Let me handle it.' I was, however, suddenly faced with the reality that he was no longer going to handle things. I was. A part of me had desperately wanted him to say, 'What the hell do you know about Tony S.?' reasserting the natural order in our world. As I walked out of the room to let him sleep, I was aware it would never be natural again.

The autumn I was twenty-three, I decided not to attend our Thanksgiving dinner. I could see that it was an exercise in hypocrisy. Uncles, aunts, and cousins, who could no longer stand one another, would drag themselves to one family's home to celebrate the Pilgrims' survival.

The day before the event, while my father was resting, I repeated my refusal to attend. My mother became irate. She was not about to show up at a family circus having lost control of one of her animals. I remained adamant. In desperation, she blurted out that my decision showed a clear lack of respect for my father.

Our yelling awakened him. He came out of his bedroom demanding an explanation. I repeated her accusation, incensed by it. 'What?' He bellowed as if gored. His face reddened, his eyes bulged, and as he turned on her, she thought he was going to have a heart attack. Her strategy in shambles, my mother retreated, begging him to calm down. I went into my room.

A while later he knocked, and came in quietly. He sat down beside me on the edge of my bed. 'I want you to know something,' he said to me softly, 'No one will ever come between us. No one.'

Before he submerged into a coma, he slept more and more, and he slept deeply. His breathing was ragged. I would stand by his bed, and call to him. Gradually he would surface from the depths, and struggle to open his eyes. Seeing me, he would raise an arm, and as I leaned in, he'd hold me around the neck.

Soon, my calling had to be louder, to get his sinking attention. Finally, shouting at the top of my voice, I could no longer reach him.

White whiskers covered his face. The beard was like a miraculous filter, eliminating age and stress. He began to look startlingly youthful. The tension in his face seemed to have disappeared, replace by a placid boyishness that was gentle, delicate, and strange.

Why I decided to shave him, I am not certain. I remember hoping that the sound of his electric razor, the familiar feeling of it on his face, might make him smile and open his eyes again.

Perhaps I needed to recognise him, disturbed that he looked more like somebody's son than my father.

As the humming blades moved slowly over his cheeks, I became uneasy. Shaving my father, I suddenly felt as if I were trespassing.

I finished. He had not opened his eyes, and I realised I had made a mistake. Without the beard, he looked like a dying, old man.

When he finally stopped breathing, the stillness was shocking. That night, the sound of the world changed.

Two clichés arrived with slicked-back hair, in black suits, white shirts, black ties, white socks, black shoes. It was three in the morning. There was a casual, business-as-usual air about them, dusted over with fake consolation, fake solemnity. Before they went in to him, they suggested that the family remain in another room when they were ready to depart, so as not to witness the exit. I told them to get on with it.

They emerged shortly with a black body bag, strapped upright to a two-wheel dolly. They rolled him out the front door like a piece of furniture.

I took a taxi home, and stared out at streets I had walked every day. Nothing was familiar.

When we brought our first child home from the maternity ward, my father celebrated by taking the infant in his hands, raising her to his face, singing and dancing cheek to cheek with her, around the apartment.

Our second daughter arrived just ahead of a massive snow storm. Her grandparents immediately drove to the hospital along treacherous roadways to get a glimpse of their newest prune-face.

By the time my son appeared, my father had vanished. It was an early August morning, three months after his death. A year before, during his illness, with no one around, I sat on the staircase in our house and said aloud, 'Dad, don't leave me alone . . .' then I heard myself finish the sentence, 'with all these women!' Now I had been joined by a baby boy.

The hospital was just across the bay from their summer cottage. Had he been alive, he would have jumped on the next ferry, and met me. We would have celebrated another link in our chain with a massive, high-cholesterol breakfast.

The morning heat descended, and I walked alone down the main street of the town, searching for a decent cup of coffee. As I walked, I kept imagining the moments of our lost celebration, the roar, the hug, the walk, the meal. Here I was, thrilled with a son, devastated without a father.

Can our children possibly see the flaws in us that we struggle with, that are sometimes an unbearable weight? Or are our short-comings magnified in their eyes because they see us with such 'size?' Is it the fate of fathers to be heros or villains, with no middle ground?

Throughout his illness I had braced myself for a sudden change in his character, an eruption of the unfamiliar, a secret face revealed by his anguish and pain. Why was I looking for a person I feared he might 'really' be, an angry stranger, who had never been exposed to me? Was it because his goodness of character was unfathomable? Was it Oedipal, the guilt of childhood, looking for relief? I do not know. What I do know is that he never changed. He was who I thought he was, who I needed him to be.

It's almost eight years later now. I'll catch an expression on a daughter's face, and suddenly wish he could see her. I'll hear a funny story, laugh, and like a ricochet of my own laughter, I'll hear his laugh come back to me. When I raise my voice to my son,

I sense my father over his shoulder, shaking his head at me.

I keep telling myself that it's the polite, reserved, unfriendliness of the small town we live in, the good friends I haven't seen for too long, the disappearance of youth, the tribulations of my career, that keep me feeling as if I am missing something crucial in life. The truth is that the world is a stranger place without him, and I am wandering in it.

STOKOWSKI'S SOCKS

CHRISTOPHER RAWLENCE

Up here, at cruising altitude, close to the flaky whitewashed ceiling of this cottage living-room where daddy long legs dance, we are edging our meticulous slow way from chair to bed. His breathing comes fitfully, each breath caught by the sheer difficulty of what we are engaged in. The window is open. The road butts right up against the house. Geoff-from-the-Caravan-Caff's Cortina just roared past, returning to the council houses from an evening down at the Greyhound. The rattle of his tired engine recedes. The soft rush of water on the weir behind the mill reaffirms itself. Untuned exhaust fumes drift in through the window, sullying the grassy air of this English summer night.

I am the navigator. We have left the familiar focus of the fireplace and for a long time now we've been crossing an unmodulated ocean of parquet. At long intervals the monotony of our crossing is broken by the aluminium flash of his walking frame as it passes back and forth beneath us. There's a coastline ahead. Far below I can make out the approaching fringes of the old Persian rug, and beyond it the woodwormed feet of the oak desk, the bottom drawer of which is still half open from my rummagings through it earlier today.

It had been raining and I'd felt that hemmed in restlessness that revisits me from childhood now and again. So after lunch, while he nodded off in the armchair and my mother zizzed upstairs, I nosed through old photographs and poked at the flotsam of their past.

On top, *The Instructive Picture Book of Quadrupeds*, Edinburgh 1860, stared up at me from my father's father's father's childhood. A lion and lioness shared the cover. I joined them at the mouth of their cave (home) and we gazed out from the darkness on to a palm fringed paradise. It was a musty old volume. I ventured inside and leafed through coloured engravings of Yellow Throated Sloths, Ornithorhynchus, Rib Nosed Baboons, each one defaced by century old infant scribblings of warriors with swords and shields.

I had just left the Dendrologus of Borneo for the Wombat of Van Diemen's Land when a flimsy bookmarker fell out and floated down on to my foot. It was a weak carbon copy of a typewritten letter dated Heidelberg 19th August 1898. 'Gentlemen,' it began, 'Der last two pags of Koffy wot you sended us vos mixed mit Rat Schitts. Der vas some mistakeneness. Ve prefer that you send us der Rat Schitts in von sack and der Koffy in annuder, and ve vill mix it to suit our gustomers. Jacobs and Schultz.'

I took a while to make sense of it. An anti-semitic joke, kept by my grandfather, the work of bored stockbrokers, passed sniggeringly from desk to desk around some city trading floor before the First World War. As I finished deciphering the crypto-Yiddish jape my father jerked semi-conscious from his head lolling snooze.

'Wha . . .?' he attempted, meaning, what was I looking at.

'The Beaufighter,' I lied, picking out an old photograph at random from the drawer.

He let out a long audible sigh. 'Dear old Beau,' he muttered, in one of the customised clichés that somehow gets past his devastated speech mechanisms. Then his head dropped forward and he dozed off again.

It was the crashlanded Beaufighter, propellers bent, marooned in some Dorset field in 1943. The bedraggled crew were lined up in front of the wrecked aircraft, smiling sheepishly, relieved to be alive. He was standing in the centre of this scruffy team photo.

His uniform was baggy, cap jauntily askew. One arm was draped round the local publican, while the other raised a celebratory pint. They'd only just made it, so the story went. Out over the channel they'd run suddenly low on fuel. A mile or so from the coast the engines had cut and, reluctant to ditch, he'd glided the machine towards rapidly approaching cliffs, just managing to nudge her up into the field. Sabotage, they'd suspected, but lately I've come to wonder whether perhaps they'd taken off without full tanks, or for some drunken reason had found themselves unaccountably off course.

Then, down among a cluster of old fish hooks and broken watches, I came across something I'd missed on previous rummagings, a rusty staple holding together several duplicated sheets marked Confidential. 'Many flights carried out by the Luftwaffe,' the top secret document began, 'are made at high altitudes in fine weather. Above 25,000 feet a phenomenon occurs which makes the detection of our aircraft much easier. The problem of the formation of condensation trails has been the subject of numerous theoretical and experimental investigations by E. Schmidt of the Luftfahrtforschungsanstalt, Hermann Goering, and others, in some cases with the support of the Deutsche Akademie der Luftfahrtforschung . . .'

It was a treatise on vapour trails. A photostat of the German original was attached. The document was a piece of low level intelligence, disclosing what the average Luftwaffe pilot knew about those tell-tale white lines in the sky, and more significantly, what he did not know.

Now, high above the Persian rug, I want to ask him about vapour trails and aeroplanes. I want to quiz him about anti-semitism, how it drifts down the generations intangibly. But I won't even try because he is incapable of voicing an answer. The most I could hope for is the joke, the resonating ditty I've heard so often before, which he might stumble out with a stroke-scrambled grin.

'There were three Jews from Norfuck, from Norfuck, from Norfuck, fuck, fuck!' is all I can recall. What a terrible beginning. Its familiarity has disguised its barbarity for me over the years. Should I ask him about it? 'Dad,' I might begin provocatively, 'I don't get the connection between Jews, swearing and fucking. What's the joke?'

And he would hear, and comprehend, and his evasion might be to ask after Miss Israel, his nickname for the Jewish woman I am then living with, by whom I have, yes Dad, a half Jewish daughter. And I would understand from his affectionate jibe that since the Six Day War he has gained altogether more respect for Jews. Didn't they win against overwhelming odds, he would reason, the few against the many, just like us against the Luftwaffe? Haven't they got a place of their own these days, where they're turning the desert back into the Garden of Paradise? A far cry from those wheeler-dealing Jewboys in the city before the war, wha?

But I won't broach these questions. Even if he could frame a reply, which he can't, it would take us too close to the gas chambers. And worse, it would face me with my own anti-semitism, his special gift to me, the jokes, the intangible sense of otherness conferred on a people utterly unknown to me in boyhood, yet who for some hazy reason I understood to be everywhere.

Well, not entirely unknown. There was Mister Levoi, my grandfather's secretary, the Jew in the heart of the family business who controlled the purse strings. 'Levoi' you called him, rhymed with boy, as if to emphasise his station. But I've since discovered he was a partner and held the company together. You told me that his name was an ineffectual attempt to disguise his true name, which was Levi – too obtrusively Jewish. And as I struggled to grasp why anyone would want to deny their origin, I absorbed your sense of the man as a necessary parasite, a benign tumour to be tolerated. I became infused with your smirking mistrust, the unstated inference that, for all we knew, Levoi indulged in a little, you know, fiddling of the books. Major fraud even. No proof, mind.

That's better. I like giving this skeleton an airing. It encourages all kinds of twisted memories out of the cupboard. Another of your ditties is now surfacing. 'Down the road there came a Jew, a filthy stinking hook-nosed Jew', it began. That's all I remember, a first line of some Jew-hating rhyme that doubtless had the city slickers guffawing in their youth.

So what on earth, I want to ask now, persuaded you to vacate that city desk for an hour or two one lunch-time, you once told me, to join the crowds against Mosley on Cable Street? Did your dislike of Hitler eclipse your aversion to the Jews or was this just an excuse for a piece of harmless rough and tumble? How did anti-fascism and anti-semitism coexist in that now dimming consciousness of yours?

We are passing the flicker and drone of *News At Ten* where Alistair Burnett is summarising a deepening oil crisis. The newscaster's craggy complexion is obscured by the slow moving dome of my father's bald head which is forming a vapour trail of straggly wisps of grey hair in its wake. There's a hazard approaching. 'Mind your toe on that fold in the rug.'

But my warning comes too late and his limp hush-puppied foot gets stuck in the stringy weft. I instruct him to lift it and am instantly aware of the foiled chains of command as they shuttle ineffectually, brain to foot, foot to brain, and again.

After several attempts he pauses and drifts away somewhere. Perhaps he's flying again, flying so high that even the Merlin is labouring. In spite of the supercharger, the Spitfire's engine can't get enough air. Nor can he, which is the whole point of the exercise. He has orders to go on climbing until he begins to lose consciousness. No oxygen mask allowed since the whole point of the exercise is to find out when the test pilot will black out.

At thirty-five thousand feet he's feeling dreamy. Miles below it's eight octs cloud. An eiderdown of stratus covers the Cambridge flatlands. Up here the diamond glint of the sun in the mirror keeps threatening him with a migraine. He holds the stick back willing the aircraft to purchase just that fraction more height in the thin air. The engine sputters, misfires, hunts for the oxygen he is quite delightfully denying himself. Come on old girl, take me up into the blue, spin me into that sweet place where nothing matters and the azure canopy wheels gracefully above, coddling, soothing, spiralling me back to the bank of some Surrey brook where all afternoon I'll fish for roach in long grey shorts, munching my way through greying doughball bait, watching for the dip of the float.

Is that where he's gone? Quite likely, because back at the armchair Len Deighton's *Fighter* lies half open on the floor, next to the much thumbed *Hardy's Angler's Guide*, 1925.

I too once fished for roach on the banks of Surrey brooks. He would lend me a rod and the special Hardy reel with the strictest instructions not to lose it. *The* Brook, as we called it, was a brown feeder of the Medway. It lay on the edge of our farm, sluggishly draining the heavy clay land that made each harvest like a latter day Passchendaele, with combines and tractors stuck to their axles in mud in the gateways of fields where the wheat lay hopelessly flattened.

These days, The Brook is directly beneath the flightpath of nearby Gatwick, which in my childhood was little more than a few sheds and a potholed runway. A few months ago I left from that same airport for New York. As I boarded an ageing 747 I noticed that the far starboard engine was unlike the others. Its snout was pale and I recalled that a month or so earlier a 747, same vintage, same airline, had had an engine failure on takeoff, far starboard. Half way along the runway, engines at full thrust, a dull bang had set the warning lights flashing. The pilot was 'go-minded', as they say, meaning that in such an emergency he realised there was no turning back, resisted the temptation to apply sudden reverse thrust and the brakes, knowing that the inertia of four hundred tons of metal, flesh, and high octane fuel travelling at 150 knots is not easy to slow. So on he went, coaxing the now three-engined machine to its limits, utilising every yard of a runway that was dangerously short, getting lift at the very last moment, retracting his undercarriage immediately for fear of fatally clipping an approaching row of trees.

They made it. The lumbering aeroplane gradually gained height and for a few hours dumped vast quantities of fuel over the farmlands of Surrey, losing weight in order to land safely.

We too lumbered along the short runway that day, all four engines screaming, in what I feared was the same aircraft, with a replaced starboard engine. As we passed the point of no return, bins rattling, wings flapping from every bump on the runway, I strained for the tell-tale thump which would indicate a repeat performance of the crisis, just for me. But the sound never came and within seconds I was looking down at my Brook, holding the palm of my right hand to my nose, inducing the heady cunt smell of fresh fish slime and the glimmering image of dried scales on my fingers.

A memory took form in the aroma, spiralling out like a genie from a rude pressure point somewhere in my nostrils. Down there, yes, right there, on the banks of The Brook, I have been fishing for an hour or two when Michael Hawkins shows up with his brother.

'Caught much?' he asks.

I point to three dead fish, drying on the grass, their mouths bloody and torn from where I have ripped the hooks. He wanders over to them, picks one up and throws it back into the brook.

Michael Hawkins is bad. He lives in the council houses, picks his nose, and turns on the milking machine just for fun when my father's not looking. 'Can I lend your rod?', he demands. I hand him the rod reluctantly, too small to resist, but aware of his grammatical error. He retreats into a huddle with his brother. A few minutes later he returns, all false hangdog and guilt. 'The reel fell in the water,' he announces. 'You didn't fix it proper.'

They leave me stunned. I stare at the swirling brown water in the futile hope of sighting the special reel, too naïve to realise it's been stolen.

The clunk of the undercarriage retracting brought me round. The engine roar dipped and the 747 turned to head for the west. Then I noticed that the sun was still shifting long after our course should have been set and it dawned on me that we were circling.

The fuel began gushing from the wing tip just as I looked out of the window. 'Some of you might have noticed,' the captain crackled through the PA, 'that we've begun dumping fuel. A passenger has had a heart attack and we have no choice but to land. I can assure you that this is not a technical fault. There is absolutely nothing wrong with the aircraft.'

So the farm that was once ours got its second toxic soak in a month, and my Brook shimmered with the tell-tale spectra of hydrocarbons. But we landed safely. The fields that had once been ours came up to meet me again, just as forty years earlier, in the cockpit of that Spitfire, half an hour after he had lost consciousness, oxygen starved at Angels 35, he awoke to see traffic a hundred feet below him and recognised the A30 near Salisbury. The Spit had flown herself beautifully, gradually losing height, perfect trim, until he came to just in time to heave the stick back, give the Merlin full throttle and climb to safety.

Stories. War Stories. Should I verify the details? Should I traipse to some bookshop and check the flying characteristics of the Spitfire? Should I leaf through the pages of a book on World War II armaments and confirm his tale that some young pilot, not him, actually could have shown his girlfriend the cannons on a Tempest one day, pushed the buttons and, Oh Christ, the fucking thing's loaded, and a burst of cannonshells makes meat of three squadron leaders in the officer's mess.

Should I look up the dimensions of the air intake of the Typhoon and confirm the plausibility of the story of how he got into a dogfight with some Hun, knocked him out of the sky, landed proudly, engine misfiring. 'Score Banger?', asked his sergeant. 'One,' he says jauntily, thumbs up, 'but the engine's playing up. Maybe he hit my fuel line.'

'Not the fuel line, Banger,' the sergeant replies, 'Take a look at this.' And there in the intake sits the red bony mass of the German's pilot's head.

How I thrilled to these yarns. What a hero he was, that test pilot fighter pilot daddy of mine. How proudly I recounted all the details to my friends. Like the time he took a Lanc up from Boscombe Down to drop dummy bombs on Salisbury Plain, when it's all drunken laughter as they lift away over Stonehenge, gin soaked from that lunch, fumbling with the first aid box for a booster of Benzedrine only to find someone's been there before them and the fucking tin's empty, but they're too tight to care.

'Look down there,' says the navigator pointing out a herd of deer running across open moorland. 'Bombs Away!' shouts Archie, the bomb aimer, and by some stroke of luck a one ton cookie falls slap into the middle of the frightened animals. On the way back, drunker now because someone has brought along a bottle of scotch, they buzz the Pheasant, their local. 'Bombs Away!' Archie bellows again and presses the release button and, Jesus, there's still a bomb on board, or rather there isn't now because it's falling rapidly towards the pub where it lands in the car park and blows every window out of the building. Still, chaps, ha, ha, venison for a month now, what?!

Shall I authenticate these tales? Would I prefer each one documented? No. Let me keep them as myths, encrusted with my image of the man.

My aeroplane stories pale beside his. No crash landings, windsheers, or hijackings. Just the heart attack incident on the 747 and a mid-Atlantic fright some years earlier when once again, I noticed the sun slowly shifting from the port to the starboard side of the aircraft. 'Ydrolico,' the steward shrugged nervously and for the three hours it took us to get back to Madrid I fantasised about fractured pipelines, incapacitated control surfaces and an undercarriage which might not come down.

It looks like we're turning back tonight. His foot is still stuck in the rug and now he's farted, a long echoing clicker that seems to billow the worsted of his trouser leg. This sets him spluttering with laughter. 'You're disgusting,' I tell him, tongue in cheek, and his splutter becomes a choking guffaw.

The hilarity wanes. I can feel him building up to a request. His body has tensed. He puts together two words. 'I . . . want . . .'

I no longer complete these synapse-wrecked sentences. I know what he's trying to say. He wants to shit, or rather, to try to shit for fear of being caught short in the bedridden helplessness of the night. Usually it's my mother who copes, but tonight it will be me. So we turn, a painstaking manoeuvre which requires me to move his stubborn feet manually, one by one, lifting each free of the rug as he eases himself round on the frame.

Each lift requires gargantuan effort and long rests in between. During these pauses he stares down at the rug through the bars of the frame, transfixed by the threadbare iconoclastic geometry of Persian gardens beneath him.

'Railway,' he says, lost in the schematised black border of the rug. And I dive with him out of the clouds, and we lock on with relief to the railway track that makes its way straight as a die, Roman-road like, east-west, across Kent and Surrey.

The altimeter spins anti-clockwise. At two hundred feet we level out and follow the track westwards. A slow goods train is approaching, filled with war supplies. The fireman waves up from the footplate, shaking his shovel with a one-of-us grin. We answer with a victory roll, dipping wingtips, two lost pilots now found.

We're moving faster now, father and son, on the return trip to the commode. The magenta geometry creeps past below, utterly unlike the random green patchwork of an English landscape with its familiar sightings. It's dry and dusty down there, like the skin on his shin, the gouty toe that protrudes through the hole of his grey sock, the dandruff that clings to what's left of his straggly grey hair.

What a scarred head he has. Above his right eyebrow a tight crazy paving of creases betrays the wheelchair accident. He had been recovering from polio, contracted just after the war. On the very day he found himself paralysed I stood up and took my first one-two-three wavering steps forward. A year later, now crippled by boredom as well, he began wheelchair racing with fellow polio victims. The inevitable happened. A wheel struck the kerb and he ended up a bloody mess on some Salisbury pavement.

Then there's the scar that runs across the top of his head, ear to ear, deep like some desert canyon. On this particular day he is driving fast down a hedge-bound country lane. The driver's window is open and his elbow hangs out of the green door of the Morris 1000 pick-up. He's in third, which the engine prefers, enabling him to negotiate the bends like a racing driver, when, Shit, look at that, a dog lurching out of the hedge right across his path. Does he hit it or swerve?

He has this thing with animals. Loves them. They love him. In the farm days, individual cows, Violet, Mary, Clare, would approach him at night when he whispered their names out in the fields. Strange dogs still curl up at his feet, drawn by some sympathetic take on the universe.

So naturally, he swerves wildly, anything rather than kill the poor hound. Tyres scream and the pick-up is rolling over and over, and somehow, with each complete turn his head hits the gritty road surface.

He comes to blinded, gropes weakly for the door handle. No door, so he rolls out into the sandy trickle of a recently dug ditch. He clambers up on to the road on all fours, sightless, but somehow not blind. A red curtain, warm and wet, obscures his vision.

'Help,' he says weakly. 'Someone help me.'

A woman's scream answers him. In the frustration of trying to see her he pushes at his eyes and suddenly the red drape is drawn and he can see. She is standing above him, biting a clenched fist in horror. As he moves his hand from his brow to reach out for her the fleshy curtain of scalp that's been ripped free from half his head flops bloodily back across his eyes.

He pushes it aside once again. The woman has fainted. He crawls towards her, feels responsible, sits hopelessly by her, dreading her return to consciousness. After a while the dog creeps out of the hedge and sidles over with a cowering wag. The woman opens her eyes but remains supine. The dog sits, shivers and whines. Everyone wants comfort, but there's none, so the three of them just sit there in silence, waiting for a passing car.

The pick-up had not taken its full toll. On a grey Christmas day afternoon that same year he goes fishing. He has been driving with the window open, elbow out, quarter light open, as usual. The pick-up rattles to a standstill in the middle of a field. He gets out, assembles rod and reel, threads up, ties a hook, picks a float. Then he reaches in through the open car window to shut the quarter light by pressing down on its chrome plated catch.

Absentmindedly, he puts all his weight on this catch and it snaps. Polio legs have left him unstable and he can't hold his balance. His body follows through and the jagged steel stump of the catch rips through the arteries of his wrist. Within seconds the blood begins gushing, pumped in great spurts several feet into the air. He is alone, miles from anyone, and must think quickly.

He reaches into his pockets for his car keys but drops them. They bounce off his foot and vanish beneath the pick-up. He gets down on to his knees into the puddle of blood that is forming around him. Supporting himself on his good hand he scrabbles with the bad one in the reddening grass beneath the vehicle. He finds the keys, heaves himself up.

A little dizzy now, two pints gone, he corrals his fast dispersing thoughts. Blood loss. Tourniquet. Hospital. He takes a handkerchief from his pocket, ties it round the bleeding wrist and pulls it tight with his teeth.

Then he drives, how he drives, along empty Christmas roads which are familiar and demand no concentration. And the winter clouds dissolve, like his thoughts, making way for a hot Mediterranean sun which beats down on the track.

Lap ten. The crowd roars because a Spaniard is in the lead. He lies second, hammering the big Norton down the straight for all it's worth. There's a judder of steel between his legs. The long cylinder is hungry for the rich mix of hot air and fuel which the expertly tuned carb administers liberally. He twists his wrist downwards. Tappets and timing, adjusted to perfection. Plug gap just so. No slack. All risk, as he submits to the ecstasy of sheer acceleration.

He approaches the hairpin at ninety and registers, too late, that a catastrophe is imminent. The crowd have surged on to the track to watch the leader, their hero, go by. They have not noticed him coming up behind.

Time slows. The gap closes. He knows what must be done to avert disaster yet can't do it. He hits one of the spectators who dies instantly. The force of the collision separates him from the bike which rises into the air and falls into the crowd killing two more people. He too becomes airborne, describing – I'd like to think – a graceful surface to surface trajectory, in fateful slow motion. He lands on his head thirty yards away.

For three months he lay on his back in a Barcelona hospital, all weights and traction. Unknown to him, the republican city was bracing itself for the conflict with Franco. Towards the end of that summer of 1936 he left for home on a ship. In the open bottom drawer of the desk which I rifled this afternoon there's a photograph of him lying on deck, bandaged and smiling on a stretcher.

The pick-up pulls up at the hospital main entrance. He slumps from the vehicle and crawls across a few feet of tarmac to collapse on the hospital steps.

'My name is Anthony James Rawlence,' he burbles to an astonished hospital porter. 'I've just pranged my motorbike.'

Blood flows from his wrist and begins a slow cascade down the steps. He has now lost four pints. The pick-up is still ticking over.

'I was lying second too. Damn Spaniards stepped out from the central enclosure. Didn't see me coming. Should have barriers.'

On the stretcher the story changes. 'I'm Squadron Leader A.J.

Rawlence,' he murmurs before losing consciousness. 'Some Hun's sabotaged the old kite. Ran clean out of fuel out at sea. Had to crash land the old girl.'

They pumped half a gallon of blood and almost as much morphine into him that Christmas Day afternoon. Around five they brought him home, drugged and smiling. Some family show was just starting on the TV. That evening the plan was for us all to drive over to my uncle's for Christmas dinner. The plan was not altered. The children were not disappointed. Later on, as we sat round in paper hats sharing cracker jokes, he blacked out and fell forward into the Christmas pudding. The brew of champagne, morphine and penicillin was too much for him.

The carriage clock on the mantelpiece has just dinged eleven thirty. The TV is emitting its after-epilogue whistle. We have left the rug behind once again and are out over parquet. The longed for touchdown of the armchair is approaching. If I look down at his left hand, feebly clutching the frame, I can see one end of the Christmas scar peeping round from the underside of his wrist.

What a tedious journey. It's like those Circuits and Bumps I once flew as an RAF cadet, stuck in the draughty tail of a Shackleton. Round and round we went, shaken by the thunder of the Gryphon engines. Round and round, taking off, circling out over some Scottish firth, back round to the landing approach where the trainee pilot would lightly 'bump' his wheel on the runway, before taking off to go round once again.

'Dad,' I want to say. 'Why did you go fishing on a Christmas Day afternoon?'

But an awkward manoeuvre lies ahead. I have to turn him again, and as he hovers there, impatient to land, I have to push back the armchair and replace it with the commode.

Now comes the delicate part. Deftly I undo his fly between forefinger and thumb. He tenses as the grey trousers drop to his ankles. His useless pink legs wobble with anxiety at the imminence of intimate exposure. The moment he has been dreading is upon us. I slip down his underpants, great baggy things whose whiteness, as they fall, contrasts with the purple shadow of a steel plate which presses through the waxy skin of his left shin, where it stabilises some long ago leg break. His embarrassment, as always, is tangible, so I affect the nurse's indifference as he removes one hand from the frame to cover his small prick.

I take his full sixteen stone weight, and we begin the descent to the commode seat. For a terrible moment we seem to be off course and we hang there, engines straining, inches above the black plastic. I start drifting. I'm the test pilot of that strange V-TOL prototype, the Flying Bedstead. A huge fifties crowd is watching it kick up dust, hanging magically above the Farnborough apron. Somewhere in the crowd you are explaining the principles of vertical take off and landing to your twelve-year-old son.

Another loud fart brings me back. Perhaps its blast will help stabilise our landing. Status critical. Time for go-minded actions. I cut the engines and your white bottom makes contact with the seat. Touch down. The dying whine of the turbine blades becomes your long sigh of relief.

'Do you remember the time you got stuck?'

'Wha . . .?'

Thirty years earlier my mother painted the old wooden lavatory seat blue and he sat on it before it had dried.

'You got stuck!'

And it's true. The buttocks that are now overhanging the seat rim were once a delicate cornflower blue. It took several bottles of turpentine and two hours to free him.

I'm not new to wiping his arse. The first time was when he got caught short on some trip we were taking to the West Country. Within seconds of a disaster we pulled into a transport caff. I parked between towering Fodens and Leylands. It was raining. Inside, the walls perspired with chip fat and nicotine. A driver was hunched morosely over a pint mug of tea, while two others played an old pinball machine perilously close to its tilt.

The gents was a tight squeeze for two. The seatless bowl was flecked with dried urine splashes. I lowered his trousers and he subsided on to the cold sticky porcelain. The usual scribbled exhortations leapt from thin plywood walls: 'I want to lick your bum hole', 'Ever had cock fun in the cab of a Volvo?', 'My wife fucks niggers while I watch,' and so on.

I looked up to find him laughing at a badly drawn pair of buttocks flanking an arsehole which was an actual hole in the wall, neatly plugged with a small ball of Bronco.

His speech was more fluent in those days. 'I once looked through a hole just like that one,' he said, 'and saw an eye looking back at me.'

'What did you do?'

'I spat at it.'

His confession sent me spinning back to the lockless cubicles of schooldays where a handkerchief through a hole in the door meant 'occupied', where the veiled smell of shit mingled with disinfectant was the olfactory ambience for afternoons of lonely masturbation, where, squatting, I'd cool my hot balls on the cold china and spurt guiltily into the bowl, where the smell of sperm on my fingers became imbued with the hovering farts of others, where the chloric edge of Harpic crystallised the imprint of my first orgasms in some place between the clinical and the unclean.

A heavy diesel clattered into life just outside the open window. A chain was pulled in the next cubicle. The transport caff gents had also had its share of jerking off. Between the thumbprinted shit smears and graffiti were the distinctive dried courses of splashed ejaculate which had dribbled down the wall.

93

'Are you finished?'

'I suppose so,' he said reluctantly.

I hauled him up and tore off several sheets of the harsh paper. He tensed immediately. It was with great difficulty that I forced his clenched buttocks apart and fingered ineffectually at his shit.

'Relax,' I said, grinning, 'or we'll be here for ever.'

This made him start rocking with laughter, so I gave up on his dirty bum, hitched up his trousers and inched him back to the car.

I'm in luck tonight. False alarm. He has sat on the commode for at least twenty minutes with no result. No bum to wipe, so I haul him up once again and he clings precariously to the frame while I reach down for his pants and trousers.

On the way down I pass his penis. It's just like mine, small and circumcised. We're roundheads. I once asked why they butchered us in this way and was told that some baby boys have overlong foreskins which grow over or clog up or are an over-tight pullback when the penis is erect. These boys are better off without it, we were informed in a sex talk at school.

I don't believe this. The roundheads in the school showers easily equalled the cavaliers. How could so many baby boys have had tight foreskins? No, I think we were ritually butchered, a razor sharp snip at that delectable place, the place of finishing, the place where nature so raggedly applies the final stitches of gender in the foetal unfolding. They stabbed us there, an exquisite slicing, and the creature writhed and screamed, suffused with a pain it could not locate, enveloped in the repressive silence of a rite which neither the doctors nor the parents rendered conscious, a rite masking as medical necessity.

Why the silent denial? Dare I suggest to you, as I zip you up, that acknowledgement of this ritual would align us with the Others? Let's face it Dad, there's an unspoken tradition of circumcision that's handed down through we Teutons that feels untowardly Jewish.

It runs deeper. Those cavaliers in the showers, the ones with foreskins, some long and pointy, others only half hooding the round tips of young penises, these boys were different. These were my early Others, the wild untreated ones, the Cavaliers.

Cavalier. The word resonates in the feeling base of my language. There's a muddle down there somewhere because each time I visualise the word I see another – Gentile. Yet if the uncircumcised are the Gentiles what does that make me? One of the Chosen? Yet I'm no Jew.

But I sang as one. For years, every Sunday night at Evensong, just after my parents had returned me to boarding school from a precious day out, when all afternoon I had fought the steady descent of the curtain of melancholy that hung over those numerous separations, when the crunch of the Morris Oxford tyres on the gravel of the school drive and the sheen of wet rhododendrons meant another fortnight of precocious aloneness, when we'd walked to the little wooden chapel and the damp sanctity of the place had become, once again, a meagre spiritual substitute for the love that I craved, when after a hymn and the Magnificat, counterpointed by the wooden thump of the organ pump, we sang the sad meaningful one, the Nunc Dimittis, also known as The Song of Simeon.

'For mine eyes have seen: thy salvation,' it went, 'Which thou hast prepared; before the face of all people; to be a light to lighten the Gentiles; and to be the glory of thy people Israel.'

Revelation. In the heart of this Church of England service I was singing as a Jew. It was the Gentiles who were the Others and I drew comfort from the fact that it was they who required lightening, not me. 'Thy people Israel' seemed to include me. The psalm offered me a sense of belonging, took the edge from my loneliness.

Gentiles slides to Gentles in my mind. Gentles. A thousand seething gentles (maggots) in an aluminium tin, each destined to writhe on a number eight hook, to drown or be snapped up by a fish.

A thousand gentles, forgotten in your aluminium bait box, hatched in a week to a thousand bluebottles. And when you opened the tin absentmindedly, they swarmed uncontrollably into the room, settling on every available surface like some grainstripping Old Testament plague.

Gentiles. Gentles. I think I've got it. Genitals. The unclean shameful place. The penis, cock, willy, dick, diminished in my childhood by the tag 'tiddlywonk'. The joke place that even now he's trying to cover with that free hand.

Don't worry, you're hidden now, safely away in those stained cavalry twills. Besides, I won't stare. She stared though. I saw her, that woman, the farmer's wife who gazed from the kitchen window of the farmhouse and saw you naked, with me, wading into the waters of her oval pool. Mum was giving birth to my sister at some distant nursing home. I had been staying with friends, learning the meaning of 'Not half!', when you turned up unannounced one afternoon and took me swimming on a neighbouring farm. No one was around when we got there, so we went in without asking.

You saw her just as she saw you. I felt your exchange of looks, somehow more complex than simple shock, as if you knew each other. Was it a field of shame that I felt swell around you, spied naked by this other woman? Was it the scandal of exposure to a neighbouring farmer's wife? Or was there some deeper current of familiarity running between the two of you?

At last we're out on the final leg, across the parquet and the rug once again, towards the hospital bed with its pulley and mountain of pillows. To starboard, the old print of *The Battle of the Glorious First of June* is heaving into view, while to port we are negotiating a near miss of the plaster cast of the five pound brown trout that we caught in a millpool on the River Nadder.

The fish swims against a painted background of green water and weeds, an approximation of the river of your boyhood and your death. In five years time, watched by my mother and my sister from the bridge, I shall pour your incinerated ground bones from a clear polythene bag into the clearer waters of this Wiltshire chalk stream. I will watch the trout taste and spit out the grey shards of you as they drift past and mingle with the weed.

Twenty years ago, we drove to the Nadder, you and I, in that jinxed vehicle, the Morris 1000 pick-up. It was my big fishing trip with you, the special treat. We set out late and arrived late, at a Salisbury hotel where we made do with ham sandwiches at midnight and shared a room under sloping eaves.

Next day we fished in that Nadder millpool. In one hour you caught several dace while I caught nothing. I wanted to move to your spot. 'Stay there,' you said, so I stayed and gazed sulkily at my float as it moved in slow circles in the eddying pool. Then suddenly the float vanished and I felt the powerful tug of somehing far bigger than a dace.

'I think I've caught something,' I said.

You turned, saw my arcing rod and my uncertainty. I saw the gold flash of something deep beneath the surface and held on tight.

'Give me the rod.'

I handed it to you and watched you play the creature for at least half an hour. It thrashed in the landing net, it slipped and slid in the grass, then you hit it, four hard blows on the head, and wrapped it in nettles – to preserve its colour, so you said.

It was still alive, hidden in newspaper just behind us, when the water bailiff came by. 'There's a big'un in 'ere,' he said. 'Must be all of five pounds and no one's 'ad 'im yet.'

'No sign of him,' you lied. The shock wave of your guilt broke over me, and I felt the same aura of the illicit that had enveloped me at the swimming pool that day. Had we done something wrong? Were we poaching? Was it closed season?

Perhaps it was only your shyness. Because you are shy. As shy as the speckled brown trout which, you taught me, flees at the slightest movement of a human silhouette against the sky, darts for cover at the faintest vibration of a footfall on the peaty river banks above. And while we're on the subject, I never did manage to tickle a trout in the way that you suggested. Crouch down low, you said, don't show your shape. Edge towards the stream on your belly. Curve your arm out over the water so slowly that the fish won't register your movement. Hand in the water now, slowly, SLOWLY, cup the fish in your palm behind its line of vision without touching it. Then bring the tips of your fingers flickeringly, like the chance touch of weed, lovingly, on to the white underbelly of the creature just behind its gills.

There, in that special place we know so well, touch it, caress it, mesmerise it, love it. One step, two step, tickle it under there. Go on now. Don't stop. Continue, until, when the fish least suspects, scoop it suddenly from the water to flap helplessly on the river bank beside you.

From where we've reached now we can look down into the open desk drawer. At the far end, beyond the old books, there's a tangle of pike lures and fishing reels. There was a time when he devoted all his spare time to fishing. For nights on end he would disappear to remote ponds in search of ancient carp of record breaking weights. Long weekends would be spent spinning for pike on drafty reservoirs. And over the years he got to know where the trout lay in the wayward pools of West Country chalk streams.

Then slowly these pleasures were eroded as the accidents and strokes conspired to incapacitate him, until he could no longer negotiate a river bank and was reduced to casting flies in a field, from his wheelchair.

Looking back on it, the tangled fishing lines seem to have increased with the knots of his own life. There came a time, in my early teens, when neither would untangle. Even now, as we lock on to our glidepath to the bed, I can conjure up the state of the farm office just before his first stroke. The floor would be strewn with bank statements – they typed overdrafts in red in those days – and bird's-nests of fly lines and nylon, each so tightly knotted that there was as little chance of unravelling them as there would turn out to be of satisfying the bank manager.

I first heard the bad news at school. I was summoned and informed that you were seriously ill. Afterwards, as I walked down the stone staircase, dazzled by the stark sunlight that raked through the leaded diamonds of the windows, I realised that you would no longer be a father to me, or, more precisely, that I must relinquish the hope that you might one day become the father that you had not truly been.

A few weeks later I grasped the extent of the damage when, at home, you searched angrily for simple words like 'upstairs' and 'door'. So began our premature role reversal and his seventeen-year terminal decline.

This first stroke brought an end to his farming career. The unspeakable, long since glimpsed, finally happened.

During the first weeks of the bankruptcy, a minor miracle occurred. It was a balmy early autumn and a bumper crop of mushrooms materialised in the light-starved world beneath the kale leaves. They seemed to come from nowhere, these clusters of white buds in the soil, and for several weeks every morning I waded in the kale filling basket after basket with a treasure that felt like an act of God. And my trousers became sodden with mercurial dew that I shook from the leaves.

And so the farm ended. Debt collectors crawled amidst the wreckage. The receiver took notes through bifocals. Animals and machinery were auctioned for what they would fetch. Local farmers descended on the scene in search of bargains among the deadstock, which they found, in a humiliating dismemberment of everything he had tried and failed to achieve.

The strokes kept on coming. Some, went unnoticed, but not the one that occurred one early morning when he was returning from his £12 a week job as a nightwatchman at the local turkey farm, the only job he could hold down. It was dawn. Another long boring night had passed uneventfully and he was driving home in my aunt's cream convertible Morris Minor when, the doctor said later, major haemorrhaging must have reoccurred in his brain, because the little car veered clean out of control, straight into the hefty trunk of an elm. The impact was severe. His knees hit the dash, driving both femurs back through his pelvis.

This might have been the end but it wasn't. After several months in hospital he was transferred to a nursing home. It was a degrading place of the kind that are exposed in TV programmes. I visited to find him on a camp bed in the flimsily partitioned living-room of what had once been a family home. The groans of dying men were filtering through the walls. The ammoniac smell of old urine hung about the place, alternating with the stink of boiled cabbage and cheap mince.

Somehow, I don't know how, he got out of that terrible place, and returned home to be nursed by my mother. On my occasional visits, when driving him to the pub, we would pass by that scarred elm tree and I observed the curling encroachment of caring bark on the gash. Then one summer, shortly before his death, I noticed a slow withering of leaves at the tree's extremities. It was the terminal onset of Dutch Elm disease.

He is tiring now. His snatched breaths are coming faster and the pauses between each swing of the frame are taking longer. There's a mucoid rumble coming from his chest. Is this the focus of his perennial gloom? Is it the seat of his anger? Is it the phlegmy sum of his untended desires, numbed for four decades by the coursing ease of alcohol?

His breathing has always sounded fast and snatched to me. It gets caught at the top of the in-breath. He seems to hold it, momentarily, in the knot of some thwarted desire, before releasing it. Perhaps if I reached down his windpipe with a delicate pair of tongs I might locate a bird's-nest of fishing line, lodged for a lifetime in that upper thoracic cavity of special needs.

Enough of this intimate probing of a dying man. Let's twist the throttle control of that five hundred Norton round as far as it will go. Burn rubber. Accelerate out of these dark places. Put your foot down and edge the green pick-up through the narrowing gap between the bus and that oncoming truck. We'll anaesthetise the pain with speed. We'll cut off the past and tomorrow with the creamy haze of Players Medium Navy Cut.

My round chaps. What's your poison? Would you rather fur your edges with clear running gin or black out on vodka? Did I ever tell you the one about the Hurricane? Banger, the CO said, I want you to take this old girl up and test her wooden prop. The back room boys say it's too long and is setting up unwanted vibrations.

So he trundles the kite to the end of the runway, pushes the throttle lever forward. Picking up speed, he fails to notice the engineer's toolbag left on the tarmac, nor, as the tail lifts, does he hear the wooden prop clip the tool bag, neatly trimming one foot from the tip of each blade.

What vibrations? Climbing through the cloud he can't see what all the fuss is about. She's running as smooth as a bird. Revving a bit higher than usual perhaps, yes, the clock says that too, but it seems an improvement, if anything. The prop seems just fine.

I know about short props. I once tried a six-inch one on my 1.5cc ED Super Fury. I had the tiny model aircraft engine bolted down to a work bench beneath the granary where I repeatedly tested it to its limits. I'd fill up the small tank with a heady mix of ether and castor oil. Then I'd flick and flick at the prop until the tiny engine coughed into life, and as I tightened down the compression screw on the top of the cylinder, it smoothed out, accelerating to 19,000 rpm with a whine and a screech.

For hours I became mesmerised by this immaculate piece of engineering at full stretch, while around me the farm came and went. Dogs chewed at cow's placentas on the dung heap. The vet arrived to see a case of milk fever. Lorry loads of fertiliser were delivered.

My little engine ran and ran. Unlike the old engines in the graveyard of farm machinery that lay overgrown with brambles behind the Dutch barn. Looking up from my screaming Super Fury I could make out the shape of the rusting Grain Marshall, a combine that gave nothing but trouble. It was a heavy machine with chain drives that invariably broke down when the weather was ideal for harvesting. Sometimes a whole afternoon would be lost with him crawling underneath the machine, hammering at sump nuts with a spanner, replacing bent cutter bars. And when at last the machine clattered into action, the evening dew had come down or three days rain had set in, making any further harvesting impossible.

Next to the dead combine, the white elephant of a second-hand bailer he once bought at an auction. For whole afternoons he had hand-cranked its black diesel engine trying to coax it into life, but the thing never once fired, still less packed and knotted a bail.

Old engines everywhere. The one that got burnt out in the elevator fire. The old Villiers from the motor mower with the shattered big end. The ancient pump motor that needed a rebore. All useless, unlike my pearl, my E.D. Super Fury.

It's time I revealed a secret. My superb little engine was useless too, but in another sense. It never powered anything, still less, flew. I had a problem, you see. None of my planes ever really flew. For months I would struggle with balsa, bellcranks, and dope, constructing my Chipmunks and Spitfires, but when it came to flying them they all crashed. All my hard work was wrecked in a few seconds. The truth is that I could not fly them properly. I wasn't good at it. Picture me holding the control lines while a friend held the plane, engine revving. 'Let her go!' I would shout, and up she'd go, up up up, then oh no, not again, down down down, straight into the ground, another irredeemable prang.

The remorse that followed these accidents was so painful that eventually I stopped flying my aircraft, even gave up making them, and settled for the purposeless testing of engines and endless dreaming about ideal model aircraft designs.

My favourite ghost plane was the scale model Lancaster with eight channel radio control. I flew countless imaginary sorties, navigating the four-engined machine to my own Ruhr Valley at the far end of the orchard. It took just the phantom flick of a switch to open her bomb doors and drop her fake load, then I'd guide the old girl safely home.

A year or so ago I revisited the farm, which I flew over in the old 747, to find that someone had built a real aero engine test bed where the orchard had once been. The orchard was old when I was young. It had several real bomb craters, shallow traces of bomb loads dropped prematurely by anxious Dornier pilots. These grassy dips lay amidst Russetts, Bramleys, Coxes and Worcesters which had gone unpruned for decades. But in good years the trees still yielded reasonably and I would sell apples for a penny a pound to the coachloads of daytrippers who stopped off at the Blue Anchor, opposite, for a drink and a wee. Now all those bent and gnarled trees, which I climbed and beneath which I gathered bruised windfalls, had gone, given way to the turbofan roar of Rolls Royce Speys – named after the great Scottish salmon river – on test for the Fokkers and One Elevens of nearby Gatwick airport.

The farmhouse was still there when I visited, right next to the testbed-orchard, so on an off-chance I knocked on the door. A man who I took to be the farmer opened it and when I explained who I was he asked me in.

'May I look at my old bedroom?' I asked.

Upstairs I gazed out of my window, through the pines that were still there, towards the fields where after dark I would watch the lamps of his tractor, the Ferguson 20, moving slowly up and down, as he ploughed his way through the night, absent from the house, delighting in solitary drunken hard work.

Turning back into the room, which was long and narrow, I caught a memory of how odd its perspective sometimes seemed from the bed, when, lying there, I felt its dimensions hugely threatening and the sheer scale of the world compressed me through a vortex of loneliness to my singularity.

I moved to the corner where the bed had once been and lay down on the floor to dwell in the feeling for a while. I shut my eyes. The nighttime of childhood returned easily. I felt smothered by the furry depths of he room. Rumpled sheets became tangled in my legs and however much I turned I could not free myself from the cloying linen. I felt stripped, egoless, without bearings at my kernel of terror.

When I opened my eyes, the chimney breast bulged, like Mum's pregnant tum. You tiptoed to my bedside and said, 'You're going to have a baby brother or sister.'

Downstairs again, the farmer beckoned me into a small windowless space which we used to call the larder.

'You might be interested in this,' he said, pulling aside a row of muddy coats hanging on the wall. I looked and saw my name, Christopher Anthony Rawlence, scribbled in a five-year-old hand.

'There used to be an old trunk in here,' I told him, 'full of my father's old bits and pieces which I used to go through when he wasn't looking.'

And I remembered my riflings of that trunk, how it fascinated me in much the same way as the bottom drawer of the old oak desk did earlier today. There were clips of live .303 bullets, a cannon shell from a Spitfire, and a book of recognition silhouettes of German planes in that trunk. There were the perennial fishing reels and fishing lines, less tangled in those days. There was the crash helmet from the Barcelona prang, cracked where your head hit the ground. There was even an old Nazi tin hat with a still intact swastika on the side.

He is sitting on the side of the bed now, clinging to the overhead pulley. I slip off his hush-puppies then pull off his socks. Stokowski's socks. Yes, these soft woollen socks with an expensive feel belonged to Leopold Stokowski, one of the world's great conductors. Leopold Stokowski, who it's said conducted seven thousand concerts to ten million people, slipped his pink five-toed walking things into the material I am now holding in my hand. What a levelling thought.

Stokowski, you see, spent his last years in a nursing home

105

nearby, where my father goes for a fortnight every few months to take the weight off my mother. And when Stokowski died one of the nurses passed on several pairs of his socks.

I undress him and ease him into his pyjamas. What went wrong Squadron Leader? Your engines once purred to perfection, with spark plugs turned to order and fuel of just the right octane. Machines roared at your whim, accelerated you round that Manx circuit, soared you into the sky. You had 'the hands', as RAF-speak puts it. Why did the wheels stop turning? Why did my planes never fly?

What went wrong Farmer Rawlence? The dog-eared first prize certificates for Young Heifers, Spring Wheat and Ploughing are staring up from the desk drawer even now. How come you were so good at the parts yet got the whole so disastrously wrong? And what became of the great fisherman, reduced to casting lead weights in a field? And how shall I negotiate your legacy of self-hatred and sense of failure? How will I get my little engine off the workbench up up up into the blue?

A few hours later, well before dawn, a knock-knocking on the bedroom floor wakes me. He is tapping on the ceiling with his walking stick. Downstairs I find him wedged helplessly on the floor between the bed and the bookshelf. Getting him back into bed requires careful planning. His wasted limbs give me no help. His ravaged central nervous system offers no instructions. He eyes me passively as I wrestle with his elephantine inertia.

In the morning I find him motionless, his breathing so light that he could be taken for dead. But his going out is some way off yet. For the time being he is engaged in a gentle cooling, a retreat from his cold hands and feet to the glowing embers of his centre.

The imprint of a dream is still with me as I pour the milk over his All Bran. I pause for a moment, letting it reform in my mind.

Through the kitchen door I can see him lying on his back, hands crossed on his chest, to all intents awaiting the undertaker.

The dream reappears. I am on the perimeter of some wartime aerodrome long after VE Day. It is a wet moonless night. Cold rain whips at my cheeks. I am making my way across overgrown runways towards the looming hulk of a black corrugated iron hangar. One of the great sliding doors is open just enough for me to slip in.

It is like a cathedral inside, vast blackness, except at the centre where I can make out an old man in a soiled overcoat hunched over a glowing brazier. I approach him across the huge space to warm my hands. He has run out of coal and is sadly protective of the last vestige of his heat. He leans into the fire, closer and closer to the entropic withering of his source.

On the afternoon of his death, constipated for a fortnight, he will eat strawberries and cream and his home nurse will say quietly to my mother, 'That man's dying.'

On the drive to the chapel of rest I shall stop at the roadside and pull a small sheaf's-worth of barley from a field. I shall stare at you in your coffin, laid out and cold, your cheeks sinking, eyes on the verge of collapse.

The space we are in was once someone's sitting room. The makeshift altar with its electric candles is actually a mantelpiece and I can detect the shape of electricity meters, badly hidden behind crimson viscose.

'Couldn't get his teeth back in,' the undertaker will say and in the drying black hole which was your mouth I will glimpse the flash of some metallic contrivance which is designed, I imagine, to contain the unsightly swelling of your tongue.

'I'd like to put this in with him,' I shall say, waving the barley at the undertaker.

'Put anything in, 'long as it burns,' he'll reply, jovially pulling back a top layer of purple viscose that covers your wrapped body. 'Just do as you like. Now if you'll excuse me for a moment I've got to go out and sell the car. Don't want a second-hand Volvo do you?'

I tuck the barley in beside you, soily roots, insects and all. How frail you look there, as if you've shrunk. Perhaps they forgot to put back your heart lungs gut kidney liver after the autopsy.

You definitely seem smaller than I remember you. Those legs look all wasted beneath the clinging material. At your far end, two bumps signal the feet that wore Stokowski's socks. These are now my socks. I own four dark grey pairs of famous socks. They will comfort my feet and nestle in my drawer.

I lean forward, kiss your cold brow, catch the whiff of your decay. My sister watches me from beyond. Her eyes are filled with tears. In a moment of exchanged looks there is a sudden understanding of the father we have shared through the years.

So much more to say. So much crying out from the interstices of our love. Like the time, like the time when. Yet enough said. Time to leave now. Lord, now lettest thou thy servant depart in peace: according to thy word.

The undertaker's voice drifts in from outside. 'Fifty thousand on the clock. She's just had new ball joints. Did 'em myself. Engine run likes a bird. No problems. Always been a good starter, even in the cold . . .'

CHEERS DAD

JOHN McVICAR

The abiding image I have of him is the smell of whisky, which even now makes me gag. He was a drunk, an alcoholic; but not an alki – always he worked, right up to the end. He died in hospital of the secondary infections due to the collapse of his liver when I was seventeen. It was 1957. I was in prison at the time and the authorities allowed me out for five days to attend the funeral and help my mother and sister with the problems of readjustment. I remember the funeral but most of all, of those days of liberty, I remember going to bed with Nancy Taylor – who kept her knickers on all night, but instead of sex gave me my first experience of intimate affection. It was more valuable than I appreciated at the time. I guess that is the abiding memory of when he died.

I was born in 1940 and grew up in the East End of London – East Ham to be precise. My earliest memories of my father are of him working in the shop. It was a backstreet newsagent 'n' tobacconist-cum-grocers and anything else that turned an honest shilling. For instance, George – my father's name and known as such to every customer – also took in shoes for repair. Every week a shoemender would collect them in a sack and return the previous week's collection. One thing I remember about my father is how he liked to hear the sound of his shoes on the pavement when he walked. He always had his shoes soled in leather and with a steel quarter heel that clicked as he walked; whereas I always had and still do have rubber soles. Anyway that was the shop – the sort of place that Indian immigrants now run.

It was certainly a living – probably a good one in comparison with the sort of work most of his customers did. They worked on the railways, in the docks, on the buses . . . the skilled and better paid were drivers and fitters. I suppose the Marxists would classify my father as petty bourgeoisie – lower middle class. But such a classification obscures more than it illuminates. The East End was and is still full of lower-class people who work for themselves in small businesses. George was a cut above most of his customers but not by much.

Of course, I had no conception, when I was a kid, of class or socio-economic categories. All I knew was that some people had more money than others, which was desirable; but how you got it was not that relevant unless it was through being a professional sportsman. And that was the only status I aspired to. My room was postered with pictures of fighters like Sugar Ray Robinson. But there was no prestige attached to being, say, a lawyer or a stockbroker or even the sort of professions that one found in the area, doctors and teachers. I certainly did not want to work as a shopkeeper – that seemed far too menial for my taste.

As much as I had conventional goals about work, it was to be an electrical engineer. An odd ambition – I think it developed from my being interested in radio – wireless then – and fiddling around with crystal sets. The encouragement of such interests and their channelling into the idea of a career was all the work of my mother. My father was a neutral bystander really. He took no interest in what I did other than to buy me something – probably at my mother's bidding – whenever I passed an exam or did something meritorious. As much as he got involved it would be to pass some Olympian stricture like 'First you work, then you play' or 'Jack of all trades, master of none'. He intervened to discourage the bad rather than encourage the good.

Petty bourgeois or not, my father probably viewed himself as working class. I say probably as apart from some offhand

CHEERS DAD

comment he had no interest in political ideologies. What he did was read the *Daily Mirror* and vote Tory. When I was about ten or so, there was an election in which all the kids I knew supported whom their parents supported – the Labour Party. My father, I knew, preferred the Tories because Labour 'puts up taxes'. As today, party activists put stickers and posters through the door but, unlike the houses of the other kids, they were never displayed in our windows. My father would not let me put anything up and just fobbed me off when I asked why.

This kind of rankled with me, so despite his ruling I decided to advertise whom I supported and put up a blue 'Vote Conservative' placard in the window above the side-door that served the living quarters of our house. The shop itself was on the corner of a junction of a fairly busy through road and a minor road; the entrance to the shop opened on to the main road and this house door on to the side road.

As soon as my father saw the placard, he took it down, which in turn led to my mother talking to me when I came home from school about not doing things that might upset the customers. I vaguely understood; but only vaguely, and my father did not go much further in trying to enlighten me. But he did not punish me either. Indeed, he was not given to lecturing nor, for that matter, hitting his children. Running the shop and servicing his habit was probably as much as he could manage.

I don't know why he drank. I know that his father, who had been a highland crofter, also drank but I do not subscribe to genetic theories of the 'addictive personality'. Indeed, it may be that he just chose to drink. I never discussed it with him and my mother, who is still alive, never knew either. 'George always drank,' she says, 'ever since I knew him, he drank. But he wasn't a drunk.' She means that he was not a stereotype drunk who became roisterous or happy-go-lucky in his cups. He did not socialise in

113

drink, even in a pub he drank on his own. More often than not he just got sodden, which could lead to a mood of sullen moroseness that put a pall of misery on the household.

I suppose, like many heavy drinkers, when he first started he was able to take his booze and was on top of it. Gradually, though, it must have crept up on him until it became the master and he the servant. Certainly, in my early teens, I can remember him as often as not smelling of whisky when I got up to go to school at eight o'clock. It didn't bother me. That was how he had always been.

He was a small, lean man, quite quick on his feet and, when sober, well co-ordinated in his movements. He had gone bald at an early age and, even indoors, nearly always wore a hat, usually a trilby. But when he dressed up, he would put on a thedora, which had a slightly more rakish cut. Apart from this, he dressed conservatively. He liked polished, leather shoes, pressed trousers, a waistcoat and shirts with detachable collars and a tie. When he was not doing too well, there was a tendency for him not to shave so much and to wear his shirts without the collars.

He shaved with a cut-throat razor that he keened on a leather strap. It was one of the few things about him that fascinated me as a child. I would watch him shave. The stropping of the razor on a leather strap, the lathering of the soap into its white china receptacle, the brushing and working the soap into the beard, then the sweeping strokes of the razor. When I first shaved I used the cut-throat but I found after going to prison, where only safety razors are issued, that I had lost the skill. Thinking back, I rather wish I had kept his razor.

When my mother spoke about our father to myself and Janice, my sister who was two years younger than me, he was not George or Daddy but 'him'. Janice and I also picked up the term. He probably knew, which must have stung. But his and my mother's marriage was fractious and discordant with the children cast as jury in the war of the parents. After the shouting had died down – usually about drinking and the money that it cost – my mother would cuddle up to us and we to her. It was as if the jury had delivered its verdict and, by sympathising with the plaintiff outside the court, was further reaffirming its judgment.

My father could not win these conflicts, not least because he did not deserve to. But my mother was quite special too. If she was flawed, it is because of her self-sacrificing ethic: what I call her taste for martyrdom. I am of a mind that givers often breed takers, so that one person's virtue is established at the cost of another person's weakness. Yet she could not go beyond her received morality; and by its lights she was a good person, a very good person indeed. With his flaws and her virtues, he could not win on any count.

It is slightly embarrassing to eulogise one's mother and I don't do it without cringing a little. Nonetheless, it is right that I bear witness to her. There is an old photograph at her home, showing her in a crowd at a wedding celebration that reminds me of some kind of cockle 'n' whelks and knees-up-Mother-Brown do. But she leaps out from the rest like the sound of Charlie Parker does from the band in those 40s recordings. There is an overpowering look of gaiety to her that, when I look at the picture, always moves me to celebrate her spirit. To me, she was also the most beautiful woman I could ever imagine.

She is old now and, because of chronic bronchitis and emphysema, hasn't long to live. The cigarettes that blasted her lungs and now give her suffocation attacks are still smoked as enthusiastically as when she first decided that they 'soothe my nerves'. When I sit with her – often moaning about her smoking or overfeeding her dog or all the other things I complain about – I

JOHN McVICAR

doubt if she has any idea of how much I admire her, honour her. The intellectual gap between us is too wide, I guess, to convey what I feel. Recently she said to me, 'I know you love me but you don't like me.' There is a terrifying truth in her words that I don't face; but sometimes when I am sitting with her I see her nobility and beauty of spirit and I tread what Wilde calls the 'holy ground' of sorrow. Always, always she gave; I don't know of one mean act that she has done. To the end of my days I will remember her with awe for what she gave me and the rest of her immediate family but, most of all, for how she lived her life.

Yet my father arouses no such emotions. My memory of him is emotionally neutral – except in the sense that I regret the fact that when he died I did not feel grief and that thinking about him now is bereft of any sense of loss. I mourn that I have nothing to mourn.

I suppose a psychoanalyst would say that I did not identify with him; certainly this lack of identification meant that he did not influence me in the way that fathers are supposed to influence their sons. As I have already said, I saw what he did as menial and I had no ambitions to follow in his footsteps by being a shopkeeper. It is possible that my rejection of him fuelled a displaced rebellion against everything he stood for, but I doubt it. My rejection of him was open and not repressed. And if I chose to wear rubber-soled shoes, it was because they suited my needs to run and fight not because they were the opposite of my father's preference for leather soles. Similarly, with crime.

I chose crime when I was around sixteen years old. I was never a juvenile delinquent acting out suppressed hostility to my father. On the other hand, while not influencing me directly or in some Oedipal reactive sense, he still had a profound impact on my life in the way that the paternal vacuum was filled by other guides to masculinity and the manner in which his drinking blighted our family circumstances. I was a street kid and my role models were older kids who embodied the virtues of young, underclass, urban culture – toughness, derring-do, sporting prowess, a rejection of authority and a taste for trouble.

I am not sure when I first knew that my father drank but whenever that was I did not know how drunkenness was evaluated socially because it was a shock to me when I learnt how others judged it. The incident that brought this home to me occurred when I was about six years old and I still remember it vividly. Some 200 metres along from our shop, the road intersected with the local High Street. On the corner of this junction was a variety theatre or music hall called the East Ham Palace. Every Christmas, the palace hosted a seasonal pantomime and probably some time around the beginning of 1947 my father uncharacteristically obtained tickets for the show.

It was rare for my father to take me and my sister out – and the occasions when the whole family went out together I can count on the fingers of one hand. The reason that explained and justified this was the long hours my father had to work in the shop. Although he shut it between one and three in the afternoon, it was otherwise open from around six in the morning until seven at night. With the claims of the shop and the logistics of drinking, it is understandable that he had little time for family outings.

Anyway at the time he took my sister and me to the pantomime, it had been snowing and the pavements were partly cleared but slippery and the gutters were filled with slush rutted by road vehicles and cycles. The three of us were walking along – with me putting as much as distance as possible between myself and my sister, Janice, who besides being two years younger than me was also a girl. Even at six years old, I was already in thrall of peer-group standards.

When we were nearing the Palace, my father slipped and fell into the gutter. My sister and I were startled and began making moves to help him to his feet. Meanwhile a couple who were coming the other way also came to his assistance. As the man reached out to my father, his wife or whatever was her relationship to him, shrilled disapprovingly, 'He's drunk.' Her face was pinched in outrage. I felt my father's shame and humiliation, but not because I was part of him, because he was my faher, but because I felt sorry for him as a person and wanted to protect him from public disgrace. The man faltered in helping up my father but nonetheless did it. He was kinder than the woman. He then helped brush him down and they both inquired if he was all right. Obviously, they were intimating that he should not be out in his state in charge of two young children.

The incident had no traumatic effect on me. I did not brood about it nor did I discuss it with anyone, not even my sister. One of us probably told our mother but I do not remember to what effect. I think it was around this time, though, that I began to understand why on the few occasions that our father did take us out she would become wary and guarded.

There were other times when the three of us went out, probably up to when I was about ten years old, as after that I would rebel against outings with either of my parents. Real boys certainly did not willingly go out with their mothers or sisters but even fathers were suspect companions. Invariably, on these outings, Janice and I would find ourselves parked outside a pub eating crisps and drinking lemonade, which to some extent suited us but was not something my mother tolerated if she found out.

Around this time, he was moved out of their marital bed into another bedroom. I knew about sex at a very early age but didn't associate my mother and father doing it. Men put their pricks into women's quims or slits and fucked them but this was for a pleasure that was naughty or dirty and should only be done secretively. I knew too that this fucking was what led to babies. However, somehow this was disassociated from my mother doing it and, as a consequence, bearing my sister and me. Indeed, I remember protesting and crying when one of my older friends realised this and teased me about it in front of others. Such contradictions, though, were incapable of affecting my emotional commitment to seeing my mother as asexual.

Neither of my parents ever spoke to me about sex but at a certain stage in my development – when I can't remember – it was assumed that I knew all about it. Of course, the idea that my father fucked was irrelevant beside the emotional fall-out from the fact that my mother must have and my classic, lower-class Madonna complex.

This complex, however, was not derived directly from religion. It infiltrated into my personality through it being part of the lower-class culture generally. In fact, I rejected religion as I did virtually everything that adults, especially those in authority, force-fed me. As I have already noted, from an early age my role models were the older kids in the neighbourhood who epitomised the ideals of East End schoolboy culture: fighting and standing up for yourself, being good at sport, showing daring in doing things that could get you into trouble with adults. That kind of thing. Religion, in my scheme of things, was for people who had something wrong with them.

Apart from his drinking, my father was fairly conventional and where he could he enjoined me to comply with whatever standards he saw as appropriate. Perhaps there was some Calvinist strain in his background that had lost its religiosity by the time he inherited it. The values that he pushed on me were hard work, honest dealing and lawfulness but no Christianity of any kind. He did support the policy of packing my sister and I off to Sunday School, which I went along with until I was old enough to rebel, but I don't think he paid more than lip service to religion. As far as I know he never went to church nor did he encourage anyone who peddled religion.

There was a period, though, when my sister went to some religious school, but that may have been at my mother's instigation. I do know that the place was run by nuns who made her ill with their sick prohibitions and lessons. This may have been a factor in my own attitude towards nuns whom I find quite repulsive. To me they seem like scuttling cockroaches but this attitude could well derive from my own atheism and anti-Christianity, which I later developed independent of my childhood or practical experiences. I remember that both my mother and father became very concerned about Janice's overwrought emotionalism and eventually they removed her from the school. My impression is that he was quite resolute in the need to get her back into a normal school.

My father would sometimes hit me but it would be a clip round the ear or back of my legs when he challenged me about the latest wrongdoing. There was none of the ritual surrounding corporal punishment that some fathers go in for. And when he did hit me, it was not as hard nor anything like as often as the teachers did with their canes. In this area, given his background, I think he was fairly moderate, even progressive, by the standards of his contemporaries.

At seven years of age, I went to primary school. By now I was a fully-fledged street kid: I was rarely indoors and even to get me in the house for mealtimes was a constant hassle for my mother. My father remained in the shop, where he worked and drank, and did little else. Occasionally there were crises. The stock in the shop would run down, my father would become gaunter, pocket money would be in short supply. Next, there would be some kind of showdown between my father and mother, which we kids did not witness and was not reported to us. The general pattern seemed to be that my mother would borrow some money off a friend of hers, my father would forswear drink and she would be installed as watchdog for the creditor. My father would stop drinking . . . for a while. The shop would prosper, he would re-stock and pay off his creditor, then he would start drinking again.

He did not take any interest in me at all. I don't think he ever looked at any work I ever did or encouraged me in any academic pursuit. When I was about ten or eleven, though, he did come to watch me box at Fairbourn House Boys Club in Canning Town. It was probably at my mother's insistence; nonetheless, he did come and I won. I remember him in the crowd, his face glistening with pride and an alcoholic flush. However, he disappeared while I was changing, obviously, as my mother commented when we got home, to nip out to the pub for a drink. There was no escape from the drink. It was just there, like having one leg or a permanent disability.

Fairbourn House was a big number to me. Football, athletics, boxing, cricket and later rugby at school were my events. I was sports-crazy as a kid. (I suppose I still am and often think that I'll die chasing some kind of ball or other.) But I never had any big talent – just sufficient enthusiasm and determination to make me a big fish in a little pond. I would always make the first team in cricket, football, rugby and represented my school at athletics, boxing or anything that was going; but once it was about selection for the area or winning some regional contest I'd become one of the also-rans. Yet, I suppose there was enough there for most fathers to feel proud of and support. He didn't but I don't think I resented him for that or, if I did, it was repressed.

Curiously enough the warden at Fairbourn House was a Tory MP who was later to be convicted for homosexual offences and was sent to prison. I think he got three years. I was inside myself at the time and felt rather sorry for him as he did not use force or seem especially bad. The public disgrace must have crushed his spirit. When I was attending the club, his homosexuality was in a way a bit of joke amongst the boys. He was known as a 'bum-bandit' and his particular stamping ground was the changing rooms. When he appeared the cry would go. 'Watch your arse, the warden's about.' He would stride in like a bustling army officer groping at boys' arses on the pretence of encouraging them to change quickly.

I didn't know about buggery or what such people did; it was just something to do with your arse. But as with sex generally, my parents did not inform or warn me about it. That was left to the schoolboy culture, which seemed to do the job rather well.

The one other occasion that my father and I did go out together was also connected with sport: he took me to West Ham's first floodlit match, which I think was in the early 50s and against a Hungarian side. At the time, I was an avid Arsenal supporter and rarely went to West Ham as they were a bit of a joke side, only providing excitement in their annual cliffhanger to stave off relegation to the third division. The match lived up to the big occasion but as always my father disappeared at the interval in order to get at the booze. Insulated from the outside world meant that he was also isolated from me. Maybe with his life now skittering into its final shabby, sordid last round, he was trying to make some kind of familial connection with his son. Perhaps. I now support West Ham in what I suppose is a muddled act of homage to the last time that we enjoyed something together.

The only skill my father taught me was chess. We had chess and draughts at home and, as a kid, I would always be eager to play. I guess I was around seven years old when he showed me the moves of chess. By the time I was about eleven, though, I was able to beat him quite easily and in order to make the game more of a challenge I began giving myself an undeclared handicap. Early on in the game, I would just remove a rook – we called it a castle – from my pieces. He caught me once and asked, 'Why have you taken your castle away?' With the sort of chilling frankness that only youth is capable of I told him. He didn't say anything but showed he was stung, although it wasn't until I was a lot older that I realised how much.

I suppose it must have been hard for him indoors as he knew that his drinking made him the family pariah and as the years passed it became more and difficult for him to keep its effects hidden. His physical deterioration, the debts, the arguments with my mother all became more and more visible. As I have described he never had a relationship with me that even loosely came within the form that we associate with father and son.

Estranged from me, alienated from my mother and friendless, all that he had in human terms was my sister. He was closer to Janice, who was two years my junior and much less outgoing than me. She was in the house more and consequently, saw much more of my father than I did. I also think he spoilt her, although that wasn't anything that I was jealous of as I didn't love him and his favouritism towards her could hardly offset her status to me as a member of an inferior species. Yet the basis of her relationship to him was self-serving. She loved my mother no less than I did but by virtue of circumstances could suck up to my father and obtain various favours denied to me. This was brought out into the open in an especially savage way through a pop song that became popular in the late 40s.

In the evenings, we would always have the wireless on and the whole family would sometimes listen to the popular variety shows and sitcoms. At the time I am talking about, the popular song of the moment was 'Daddy's Little Girl.' My sister hated the idea that she was daddy's little girl and I would use the song to tease her. She couldn't cope with challenge to her identity and, no matter how it ran against her interests, could not contain her emotional reactions in front of our father. The song came on one evening while we were all sitting in the living-room and I began singing along to it, looking at her. She burst into tears and rushed to our mother. My father just looked bemused but even then I knew that he had been cruelly exposed and I remember feeling shame at what I had done.

When I was eleven, I went to secondary school; there I had about a year of being a proper schoolboy, before being swept up by adolescence into the maelstrom of staking out an adult identity. For me, this was established by bucking the system, then crime. By now my father was just a confused onlooker to both my heady rush into the penal system and my mother's agony and bewilderment at being unable to do anything about it.

My early teens coincided with my father's late forties and it was about this time that his physical decline began its inexorable slide into death. I saw but didn't notice. He went into hospital a couple of times and was discharged with the usual warnings that chronic alcoholics receive. Of course, he didn't stop drinking. I was sent to prison in 1957 – I served twenty months – and that more or less ended our relationship. He never visited me and wrote only once. The letter was the result of my mother attempting to affect what I suppose she thought was some kind of reconcili- ation, but we had never known or felt for each other, so there was nothing to reconcile. His letter was just empty platitudes about him hoping I was well and would be released soon. I replied but we were two strangers trying to be friendly. I think he only wrote the one letter.

I never saw him again – not even in death. He died in 1968, aged fifty-four. The prison authorities paroled me to attend the funeral and help with the family business. At first it was for two days but I managed to get the leave extended to five. The funeral was just a funeral to me. I felt nothing and saw even less. I never looked at his corpse. He was cremated and his ashes are presumably still held in the cemetery that lies opposite Wanstead Flats. I doubt if I'll ever go back to see – but I have given this to my own son, who was born some ten years after George died, to read.

THE MAN WITH THE BRIGHT RED TROUSERS

JOHN HOYLAND

When my father went to war in November 1943, he wrote to me at least once a week – usually several times a week – for the next year. I still have the letters. They are all on army notepaper, with just his name and regiment at the top, written in block capitals as instructed: "Lt D. HOYLAND, R.A., 76 (R.W.F) A, TK REGT, RA, B.N.A.F." The major part of each letter is taken up with a drawing in coloured crayons, and down the side and around the drawing, again in block capitals, is an instalment of a story.

I look at one of these letters at random, and find a picture of an orange tree with a bucket of lemons under it. A hedgehog has fallen off a cliff in a previous episode, and has landed in the tree. My father writes:

DEAR JOHN, HERBERT THE HEDGEHOG LANDED RIGHT SLAP INTO THE MIDDLE OF THE TREE WITH A SIMPLY TERRIFIC CRASH, AND, OF COURSE, BEFORE YOU KNEW WHAT HAD HAPPENED HE HAD GOT TWO ORANGES STUCK RIGHT INTO HIS OLD PRICKLES! – DAD.

That's all, until the next letter, which will be another equally brief episode of the story.

When he ran out of stories of his own to tell me, he told me the story of Peter and the Wolf, and his drawings of this – the mean, rangy wolf, and the plump self-satisfied duck – are among the most delightful he did.

There is nothing in the letters about my father himself – what he was experiencing, what he was feeling, even where he was – though the drawings of orange trees and olive groves make it plain he was in the Mediterranean, and one letter consists simply of a drawing of two gaudy and very un-English butterflies he had seen: DEAR JOHN, I SAW TWO LOVELY FLUTTERBIES SITTING ON SOME FLOWERS IN A WADI YESTERDAY, AND TRIED TO REMEMBER THEM AS BEST I COULD. HERE'S *SOMETHING* OF WHAT THEY LOOKED LIKE. BE GOOD – LOVE – DAD.

The only real sense I have of my father as a person is derived from these letters. From them I get the impression of a man who lived life with gusto and humour, a man with a fine artistic sensibility, a man who liked to tell a tale . . . and a man who loved me, and missed me, very much.

When my father was killed, my mother took these letters to a shop to be bound in leather. When she went to collect them a couple of weeks later, she found that the man who had bound them had got them all in the wrong order, spoiling the sequence of the stories. She was very bitter about this. Whenever we took out the letters to read, as we often did during my childhood, her mouth would pull down with anger, and she would say, with a vehemence that always shocked me: '*That stupid man*!'

It was yet another way in which fate had set out to cheat her when it came to anything to do with my father.

I was three years old when he died. Yet he was with me throughout my childhood and youth, a powerful force in his absence. He stayed at the centre of my life, ruling my head and my heart – the person I looked up to and wanted to emulate more than any other human being . . .

Now, when I try to write about him, I find I have a language problem. Do I call him 'my father', as I have done here to begin with? Do I call him 'Denys', as my mother does? Or do I call him 'Dad', as he signed himself in those letters he wrote to me from the front?

I think I shall call him Denys, for a while. So much of what I know about him comes from my mother, when I try to tell his story this is the name that seems the most natural.

Denys came from a middle-class Quaker family. On his mother's side, in particular, the family was rich, but Denys grew up in more modest circumstances. This was because his father – my grandfather – was a particularly sincere Quaker who did not really approve of possessing large amounts of money when others were poor, and who had therefore never shared much of the family wealth.

This grandfather had left Cambridge shortly before the First World War with a first in Classics. He had fallen in love with a Quaker girl called Helen Doncaster, who by all accounts was as devout and idealistic as he was. The two married, and almost immediately went to India to be missionaries, providing medical and other forms of aid to the Indian poor.

It was in India that Denys was born, along with an elder brother John and a younger brother Peter. But only two or three years after Denys's birth there was a typhoid epidemic in the area where they lived. Denys's mother and his baby brother both contracted the disease and died.

Denys's father decided to continue his calling in India on his own. He sent the two boys (Denys and John) back to England to be brought up by two of their aunts in Sheffield. Although he came to England whenever he could to visit them, effectively the two boys grew up fatherless, just as my younger brother and I did.

By the time Denys was in his teens, his father had married again, and eventually he brought his new wife back to England, where they settled in Birmingham. The couple had three more children, Mick, Francis and Rachel.

By this time Denys had gone to a Quaker boarding school, Leighton Park, in Reading – and this is where his story starts to acquire a more detailed resonance for me, because I went to the same school myself in the 1950s.

As Denys's eldest son, I inherited various bits of memorabilia about him when he died, and amongst these there is a pewter mug he was presented with when he left school. It has a glass bottom and two ornate handles, and the dull grey metal is engraved with the school shield and a list of my father's achievements. Amongst other things, it says that he was captain of rugby, captain of cricket, captain of fives and captain of athletics. Other records about him state that he was also a first class scholar and was very artistic.

The problem for me when I went to Leighton Park was that all this was an extremely hard act to follow. I could just about manage on the academic side (though always suspecting my father had been a lot better than I was in this as in everything else), but the sports side of things was beyond me. To make matters worse, for my first two years at the school the sports master, who was known familiarly as 'Hoppy', was the very same man who had taught my father twenty-odd years before. He talked about Denys in reverential terms as the best athlete the school had ever had, and quite plainly expected me to be a chip off the old block. For those first two years I sweated blood trying to live up to his expectations, and I am convinced to this day that Hoppy drove me harder than any other boy in my year, simply because he could not understand why Denys's son wasn't the toughest rugger-player, cricketer, runner and jumper in the field.

Around the time Denys left Leighton Park, his elder brother John was killed in a climbing accident in the Alps.

By all accounts, John was an outstanding young mountaineer, and the family lore is that he had been selected for a future British Everest expedition. His father's cousin, T. Howard Somervell, had already climbed to within 1,000 feet of the top of Everest in the fateful 1924 expedition in which Mallory and Irving were killed. Mountaineering was a passion in the family – one which Denys also shared.

John was climbing with a friend on the Inominata Ridge on Mont Blanc when the two of them fell off to their deaths. Some say the climb they were attempting was too difficult, given the poor weather conditions at the time.

When it was realised John was missing, my grandfather went to Switzerland to join the search for him, and one of the grim mementos I eventually inherited from the family was a photographic record of that sad search. The photos showed my grandfather dressed in climbing gear, still a very handsome man in his forties, his mouth grimly set and his face shuttered with grief and anxiety. With him was Frank Smythe, the great Everest climber, who led the search for the two young men. Behind them in the pictures were the crags and snow slopes of the Alps, darkened by cloud. Several of the photos were of the cliff that John and his companion fell down, and one of them showed a snow scree-slope at the bottom with an arrow pointing to it and a note in my grandfather's scratchy handwriting saying: "Bodies found here."

Sadly, I can only describe these photos in the past tense. I remember them quite vividly, but I am unable to refer to them directly, because at some point in my youth – I don't even know when – I lost them.

After Leighton Park, Denys went to Balliol College, Oxford, to read History. While he was there, two important events took place in his life. One of these was that he broke with his father's Quakerism and joined the Communist Party – a move he had apparently been contemplating even while he was still at school winning athletics prizes.

The other event was that he met my mother.

133

Theirs was a cross-class marriage.

My mother's father was an engineer in the Chatham dockyards. He had served in the Royal Navy in the First World War. After a disastrous and childless first marriage, he married again in his middle age, to a woman much younger than himself.

Though he brought home a regular wage, which made the family better off than many in their community, there was little to spare, and my mother's childhood was extremely tough. Of her seven brothers and sisters, three died in childhood, and when my mother was thirteen her mother walked out of the house with another man, and was never seen again. My mother, as the only girl, became the one who looked after the rest of the family.

At sixteen, she went to work as a shop-assistant in a London department store. She was bright, and her school wanted her to stay on. But she was a working-class girl, and the family could no longer support her. In those days, there was little choice in the matter, especially if you were a girl.

With her father's agreement she moved into a room in London in a hostel run by the department store for its salesgirls. Her father was a trade union man and a socialist, and sufficiently broad-minded to give his daughter his blessing when she left home to make her own way in the world.

Conditions in the shop where my mother worked were very bad, so my mother, taking a leaf out of her father's book, started to unionise the girls. There was a successful struggle over working hours which brought my mother to the attention of the union and, before long, the Communist Party.

She joined the Labour League of Youth and (secretly) the Young Communist League, became an activist, met intellectuals and artists, and ended up working full-time for the League of Youth's journal, *Advance*. She left the hostel, with its strict rules and regulations, and took a series of flats with a girlfriend. There were evenings spent talking till the small hours, people calling day and night, arguments about politics, about unemployment and the rise of fascism.

One summer, when she was nineteen, she went on a Labour League of Youth summer camp. On the second day there, the campers were joined by a group of Communist students from Oxford. My mother happened to be at the gate when they arrived, and saw them coming down the road. One of them had flaming blond hair with a handkerchief knotted over it, and a pair of bright red trousers. She knew the second she saw him that this was the man she would marry.

They fell in love with each other there and then, and for the next year she visited him regularly at Oxford. He used to smuggle her into his room at night so that they could sleep together. Or he would come down to London, and they would meet up with friends, usually to go on marches or to meetings – they were on the great anti-fascist demonstration in Cable Street together. And there was a holiday in France with another couple, student friends of Denys's. The four of them spent the evenings reading books aloud to each other, until the other guests in the hotel complained and they had to stop.

After he got his degree, Denys spent a year doing a teacher's training course in Birmingham. My mother continued to visit him at the weekends, and, for the first time, she met his family. As Quakers, they believed in tolerance, and in formal terms did their best to make her welcome. But she was working class and she was a Communist and, perhaps worst of all, she wore make-up. She was decidedly not the kind of girl they had in mind for Denys. So the tension was never far beneath the surface, and there were occasions when the politeness broke down completely and there were fierce political arguments with Denys's father.

In 1939, Denys moved to London, and he and my mother

married in the early summer. They had a two-month-long honeymoon, much of it in Edale, in the Derbyshire Peak District, which provided my mother with a gentle introduction to the Hoyland family's love of mountains. On their return to London, they moved into a flat near Highgate, and Denys started working as a teacher at a primary school in Kings Cross.

It was a happy time, but now there was a terrible shadow over their relationship. Only a few days after their marriage, Britain declared war on Germany. Hostilities did not break out immediately, but my parents' lives, like everyone else's, became extremely unsettled. And in May 1940 – after a period when the children Denys taught were evacuated to Lincolnshire, and he had to go with them – Denys was called up.

His agreement to join the army was passionately opposed by his father, who was a conscientious objector. But, as my mother told me, Denys believed that fascism had to be fought, and felt he had no option but to go to war.

He was sent off to be trained, and for the next year or so they only saw each other intermittently when he was given leave, or when she was able to visit him at his training camp. But the following spring he put his knee out playing football, and an army surgeon succeeded in temporarily paralysing his leg while trying to operate on it. This meant that he had to spend the following six months in hospital. He was stationed in Cardiff at the time, so my mother went there and took a room to be near him – and it was in Cardiff General Hospital that I was born.

I had been conceived during the Blitz, which my father and mother had watched from Archway Bridge, near their Highgate flat, when he was home on leave the previous autumn. In Cardiff, too, there were bombing raids when I was born.

This detail, which my mother told me, contrasts in my mind with something else she told me; when she came out of hospital

136

with me and was taken back to her room, it was completely full of wild flowers, which Denys, who had been allowed out of hospital for the day, had picked on a railway embankment nearby.

Denys's accident meant that he could have stayed with the searchlights regiment to which he had originally been posted – and which, incidentally, my mother tells me he thoroughly enjoyed (he liked being a squaddie, mucking in with the other squaddies). But he wanted to be at the front – he wanted to *fight* fascism – so when his leg recovered he applied to train as an officer in an anti-tank regiment.

He stayed in England for another two years, stationed at various camps around the country, during which time my mother moved to Birmingham. Now that she had a baby, she felt she had to accept the offers of support that Denys's family had been making, and she allowed them to arrange for her to move into a house near theirs in Selly Oak. All her friends in London had in any case dispersed because of the war, and the flat she and Denys had lived in near Highgate had been bombed.

The only memory I have of my father comes from his time. It is a memory not so much of a person, but of a smell and a texture – the smell and texture of khaki. I am in my grandfather's garden in Birmingham, and my father is on leave, and he is holding me in his arms, my face pressed against his shoulder. I can smell and feel the rough cloth of his uniform.

It is a powerful memory – but even so I am not entirely sure how genuine it is. I sometimes think that what I am remembering is not the occasion itself but rather the feelings that were provoked when I was shown the photographs of that scene in the garden.

I still have those photos, and they still move me. My father looks very young in them, like soldiers when I see them today. The uniform looks well on him – he has a tough-looking body. He looks very proud of his baby and his pretty wife, who is there beside him, clinging to his arm and peeping into the baby's face – my face.

What strikes me most is how beautiful he is. The brutal angularity of his military hair-cut – shaved almost clean right up the sides of his head – fails to dim the brilliance of his golden hair. Though the pictures are black and white and faded, he seems to blaze with colour, my father, and his eyes are so blue they seem to burn you. His face, in almost every picture, is lit up by a grin.

My mother was in the final stage of pregnancy with my brother Bill when Denys was sent to the front. He was given compassionate leave to go and stay with her for a fortnight, and during this time they both desperately hoped that my brother would be born. But she didn't go into labour until he had left on the train to Southampton. He telephoned her from there before embarking two days later, and she was able to tell him he had a second son. She never talked to him or saw him again, and Bill never met him at all.

One of the problems for the families of someone who is killed in a war on foreign soil is that there is usually no body, no funeral. Instead, in the Second World War, there was just a telegram, followed perhaps by a commendatory letter from the commanding officer, and the return of any remaining personal effects.

In my father's case, in September 1944 – a year after he had been sent to the front – the telegram was delivered, as was customary, to a neighbour, who came round to break the news to my mother. The same neighbour telephoned my grandfather, and he and my aunt Rachel hurried across Birmingham to be by her side.

'I shall never forget that night, not till the day I die,' my Aunt Rachel told me. 'How your mother cried! I have never heard such crying, before or since. She cried on and off all night. Such long, tearing sobs! I stayed with her for the night and made her cups of cocoa. It was all I could think of to do. I was only eighteen. He was my adored older brother. I worshipped him. But I couldn't express my own grief at all, your mother's was so strong.'

'I never for one moment thought he would die,' my mother told me. 'It never occurred to me as a real possibility. Of course, if your husband goes off to fight in a war, you have to take it into account. We even discussed it together, and he obviously knew there was a risk, he wasn't a fool. But I never thought it would happen. He was so full of life, it simply seemed inconceivable.'

I don't know how much she ever really accepted that my father had been killed, deep down. I think that part of her believed, for years afterwards, that they had made a mistake and that he was still alive.

Part of me never really believed what had happened either. Part of me went on thinking that he would come home. Even today, I sometimes have dreams in which I learn that he wasn't killed and that he is going to return.

But he didn't return, and his failure to do so created a great darkness in my childhood. The dominant force in my life became grief. But there was no shape to this grief, no contours to mark it out and contain it. Instead, it clung to the three of us – my brother, my mother and me – like a mist or a shadow, always there but never seen, omnipresent but intangible.

In fact, I actually remember very little of my childhood. There are a few good times that poke out of the mist, but most of it is a blank. Instead of details, I remember simply a feeling that there was an ugly hole in the middle of my life – and I remember my mother's unhappiness, and how desperately and futilely I wished I could do something about it.

Lacking a real father, I tried to invent one for myself. One shameful memory that I do remember from my childhood is being mocked at primary school after announcing that my father had got within a hundred feet of climbing Mount Everest. And it was only very recently that I discovered that the reason my father was in hospital in Cardiff when I was born was that he had had an accident playing football. I had always believed that he rode a motorbike, and had had a crash.

A tendency to dramatise my father's memory in this way was not the only problem I had in how I related to his absence. It was agreed on all sides throughout my childhood and youth that my father was an exceptionally wonderful and gifted person, and my mother's unending grief for him convinced me that this must indeed be so. To be good enough to be his son, and in particular somehow to make up to my mother for his loss, I felt under great and sometimes immobilising pressure to be an exceptionally wonderful person myself.

Perhaps all sons feel some of this desire to live up to an idealised image of the father, and perhaps all find it difficult to do so, especially if the father is a relatively absent and mysterious figure. But if the father is completely absent – if he is dead – it can be more difficult still. It is very hard to live up to such a person, because you don't have the actual person there to measure yourself against. All you have is a ghost. So nothing you do is ever going to be enough. There is a constant feeling of failing, a constant sense of shame.

And perhaps part of me didn't want to become like my father anyway. Part of me resisted the mythic voice of his authority in my head. Part of me wanted to fail, to avoid the responsibility of success, to be a 'bad' person rather than an exceptionally wonderful one. Because finally to become like my father would, in this case, mean being dead.

One way out of these traps was to dream, and perhaps one reason why I remember so little of my childhood is that I spent so much of it in the refuge of my imagination. In my dreams I became the person I felt my father would have wanted me to be. I performed great and noble deeds and was a leader of men, a protector of the weak and the misunderstood.

I was also given to dreams in which I was misunderstood myself, to the point even that I sometimes liked to dream about my own death, with people gathering round my death-bed to explain how sorry they were over the way they treated me.

But in my nightmares death took on a different face, and came rushing out of the darkness to claim me, or to claim my mother, and take us where my father had gone. My mother tells of the many times she had to come to my bed to calm me after these nightmares.

Fortunately, there were male influences on my childhood who were able to rescue me, to a degree, from these kinds of confusions about what men did in the world. Of these, the most potent by far was my grandfather on my father's side, John S. Hoyland, known to his friends as Jack.

Grandad, as my brother and I called him, was a tall, strikingly good-looking man, with a tremendously loud voice. The size and the voice are family traits: all my uncles and great-uncles were huge men with voices that boomed like fog-horns. (My father seems to have bucked the trend, though – he was scarcely taller than my mother, and compared to the others I am told he was soft-spoken).

Grandad was one of the leading Quakers of his generation. He was a prolific author, he was a lecturer at the Quaker college, Woodbrook, in Birmingham, and he was a tireless public speaker and activist. After his time as a missionary in India, he devoted the rest of his life in England to continuing the service of his ideals. His great passion when I was young was Peace, and as Chairman of the Friends Peace Committee, he spent his life driving around the country in a battered old Ford Popular, speaking at meetings and going on demonstrations. I have a picture of him in his old age speaking at a demonstration in Trafalgar Square. He seems twice the size of the Quaker ladies standing beside him with their posters saying 'Renounce The H-Bomb' – but his hair is grey, and his suit is crumpled, and his hands are clasped behind his back, and his face, with its national health spectacles and its earnest frown, is the epitome of that non-threatening idealism the Quakers call 'concern'.

A few years later I was to speak on this same platform as a member of the executive committee of the Youth Campaign for Nuclear Disarmament. Because of that photo of Grandad, the occasion had a particular resonance for me. I felt very proud of myself, doing something that I felt sure Grandad – and perhaps my own father too – would have approved of.

Throughout my childhood, Grandad tried to do what he could to make up to my brother and me for our father's loss, and we regularly went to stay in his house in Birmingham. From there he would take us off in the Ford Popular to visit great-uncles and great-aunts (including the maiden aunts who had brought my father up) in their large houses. As he drove along, he would sing sentimental ballads in a deafening, tuneless roar that had my brother and I cringing in our seats.

Grandad's own mother had died when he was a child. Then, when he grew up and married, his wife and three sons – Helen, Peter, John and Denys – were all wiped out one after the other, leaving my brother and I as the sole survivors of that first family of his. Yet despite all this tragedy and the suffering it must have caused him, he remained a man of tireless energy and enthusiasm, and a lover of conviviality.

His Quaker conscientiousness was never far beneath the surface, though. When Grandad heard what he considered to be a good joke, he wrote it down on a card he kept for the purpose, and secreted it in his inside pocket. Then, when there was a lull in the conversation over dinner in one of the country houses, he would sneak a look at the card and proceed to tell the joke, to the twittering and fluttering of the maiden aunts.

When I was about fifteen, Grandad came to my Quaker boarding school as the guest speaker at Sunday evening meeting. I remember the mixture of pride and embarrassment I felt when the headmaster led that familiar figure on to the stage and sat him down in front of all the boys in the school. After we had sung a hymn and heard a reading from the Bible, he rose from his seat and came to the front of the stage, where he towered over us like a colossus. He peered at us in silence over his glasses for a moment, then opened his mouth and thundered in that enormous voice:

'H FOR HELL AND HARWELL!!!'

His voice was so loud the entire school leapt out of their skins.

I don't know how he managed it, but his speech somehow progressed from the iniquity of the atomic research station at Harwell to the problem of Indian villages that had no well to supply fresh water. He convinced us that the girls in these villages were in constant danger of being eaten by tigers when they went through the jungle to fetch water from the nearest stream. The result was that the entire school abandoned academic work for several weeks in order to make things (like fudge and bits of carpentry) to raise money for wells for Indian villages. The whole lot was eventually sold off at a fair that raised over a thousand pounds.

By this time Grandad's hair had gone silver grey, and he had

143

come increasingly (and to my mind alarmingly) to resemble Jehovah.

At sixty he had a stroke. He was initially slightly paralysed, but otherwise made a good recovery – and ignoring the doctors' advice he went straight back to touring the counry and speaking at meetings.

He did, however, abandon the old Ford Popular, and travelled instead by train. This enabled him to take advantage of a new skill he had picked up in hospital. The occupational therapists there had taught him to make small teddy bears to help him get back the co-ordination of his hands and arms. Grandad had been thrilled to discover that the cost of raw materials was only five shillings for a teddy bear that could be sold for ten shillings.

For the rest of his life, this big, biblical-looking figure made teddy bears whenever he had the opportunity. He did it on trains, in people's houses when he visited them, even on the stage waiting for his turn to speak. He made several thousand of them, and sold them all to raise money for wells for Indian villages. I remember him sitting in the headmaster's study before that speech at evening meeting, his silver-haired head inclined over the work in his lap, his craggy, still-handsome face slightly lop-sided in concentration, his huge hands painstakingly sticking the needle into the cloth and binding it up.

He died at sixty-five, just as the doctors said he would if he didn't ease up.

I mentioned earlier that when my father died, I inherited a number of mementos of him and his family. These mementos had an important effect on me as a child. They became inextricably associated with my father in my mind even if he did not appear in them directly, and their ghostly messages reinforced that sense of doom and sadness that my father's death had bequeathed me.

This is particularly the case with a book written by my grandfather for his two sons John and Denys when their mother Helen died. The book, which was written in Grandad's hand-writing in a large notebook, was intended to tell the two boys what kind of a person their mother was. When both of them died, it came to me as the eldest surviving male of the family. One of the interesting things about it is this: although I have talked here about having a ghost for a father, I do not actually believe in ghosts, except metaphorically. In this book, however, my grandfather revealed that he really did believe in ghosts.

In the book my grandfather started by telling his sons about the early days of his relationship with Helen – their courtship and their love for each other, their decision to go to India, and their common desire to devote their lives to the service of God. He tried to give the boys a sense of their mother's personality, emphasising not only her idealism and her strength of character, but also her tenderness and her capacity to love.

It seems that he and Helen were particularly happy together in the early days in India, and one incident stood out. They stayed in Hyderabad not long after they arrived, and one day they went for a walk in the woods, pausing for a while at a bridge over a stream. They felt so peaceful and so united that day that for a long time, as they stared down at the stream, they felt no need to speak to each other – until Helen suddenly turned to my grandfather and said, in the old Quaker idiom:

'Jack, if thee should ever lose thy Helen, do not grieve too much. I believe our spirits are so united that I will always be with thee, even if I should die.'

After recounting this and other incidents illustrating the love he and Helen had for each other, my grandfather went on to describe the work with the Indian poor, and how selflessly Helen took part in this even though she was bearing children. When the typhoid epidemic started, she worked harder than ever caring for the sick, and it was this, my grandfather believed, that made her succumb to the illness herself.

It took her three or four days to die. When she was going, and knew she was going, she whispered to my grandfather (and they were her last words):

'Jack, remember the bridge at Hyderabad.'

My grandfather finished the book by telling the boys about his grief at her loss – but then he went on to say that what Helen had said on the bridge was true. Even though she had died, their mother was still with him, and with them. He knew it. He could feel her there, all the time.

All in all, it was a very moving little book, this book of my grandfather's, and I wish I could tell you more of what was in it. But I can't because I lost it.

I lost it a long time ago, as I also lost the photo album with the pictures of my grandfather searching for his lost son John on the cliffs of Mont Blanc.

There is a sequel to this story. The last time I stayed with my grandfather at his house – a year or so before he died, when I was fourteen – he called me up to his study one day.

'John,' he said. 'I am going to die soon, and I want to get rid of some of my books. I would like to know that they'll be appreciated, rather than merely disposed of when I'm gone. So I'd like you to choose four books from these shelves, four books that you would really like to have.'

His request threw me into confusion. I wanted to reply: 'Nonsense, Grandad. You're not about to die. You've got years of life in you yet!'

But I knew he was in earnest, so I started to study his shelves. He was a great reader, and had never lost his love for the classics –

one of his chief relaxations was reading Homer in the Greek. His shelves were very full, lining one wall of his study from floor to ceiling.

I found it difficult to choose, because I knew how much the books I selected would matter to him. They would tell him something about me, and they would also be a memory of him that I would take away with me. There was something a little bit creepy about this. It was as if he was already trying to talk to me from beyond the grave.

I made little attempt to choose books I genuinely wanted. Instead I went for books that I felt would please him: a book of Plato's dialogues, a leatherbound copy of *Wuthering Heights*, one of my grandfather's own books (about working with the unemployed in the thirties, and called *Digging for a New England*) and a volume of Wordsworth's poetry.

When I showed him the books I had chosen, he nodded gravely, and I was relieved that he seemed satisfied with my choice.

Years later – long after he died, and long after I lost the book about Helen – I happened to open the Wordsworth at the back instead of the front, and found a sonnet written there in my grandfather's writing.

It described a mountain scene in Switzerland. Rather surprisingly, considering my grandfather's pacifism, it started off talking about 'those cloud armies marching up the sky' and 'these tree armies marching up the slopes' – but it then went on to describe the beauty of the scenery in less militaristic terms.

It finished by saying how much more beautiful the scene was because Helen's spirit was there to share it with him.

'After all these years, as promised, thou art with me still,' he said.

I wish I had the poem in front of me now. I remember it had a date on it, and I would like to know how long after Helen's death he wrote it. I can't help wondering if he went on feeling that Helen was still with him after he had got married a second time.

But the poem is not in front of me now, because, like my grandfather's book about Helen and the photo album about Mont Blanc, I lost that volume of Wordsworth with my grandfather's poem in it.

After losing the other things, I had been particularly careful about looking after this book – but somehow or other, it went.

There was one bit of memorabilia about my grandfather's relationship with Helen that I managed to keep. When my grandfather wrote his book for John and Denys, he also wrote John, the eldest, a letter 'to be opened by himself on his seventeenth birthday'. Grandad apparently believed that it was all too probable that he too would die in India as his wife had done, and the letter was to be given to his son if this should happen. But it was John who died first, and the letter remained unopened. My Aunt Rachel discovered it among Grandad's effects in Birmingham after his death, and passed it on to me. There was also a letter for Denys, which she gave to my brother Bill.

The letter is headed: 'Tyrrhenian Sea. Nov 10, 1919.' Here is some of what it says:

My dear Johnnie.

When you read this you will be just seventeen. God bless you, my son; you will be nearly a man. How greatly I hope that you will be a good and noble man, a doer of your duty and a fighter for truth and purity and justice in the world.

I know that you are as eager as I am myself for you that you should be becoming a strong, trustworthy, clean man, Johnnie. Whatever temptations and difficulties may come, never give up one jot of your absolute resolve to be the very best you possibly can be. All through my time at College I had the motto 'The Utmost for the Highest' in my rooms, and the same one was in our drawing room and our little private chapel in our bungalow in Hoshangabad. It was the motto of the great painter G.F. Watts, and it has always seemed to me to be the best kind of motto a man can have for his life. Emerson put the same idea in the homely phrase 'Hitch your wagon to a star'. They both mean that the only chance for us to be true men is to aim with all there is in us for the very highest possible ideal. We must give all we have, all the time, for the Kingdom of God. Our self-sacrifice must be absolutely unstinting.

This sort of life doesn't give what the world calls happiness. It means often the extremity of anguish and self-denial. But if we follow it we shall be more worthy of the name of man, and of the joy hereafter. For remember, my son, there is no Death. I have learnt that great truth once and for all in the bitter grief and loss of this year 1919, which has taken from me, who began the year the head of a family of five, every one of those five by death or long separation. I want you to have a copy of my little book of poems called *The Bouquet of Death*, most of which I wrote soon after your mother died. They are poor stuff as poetry; but what they try to say is *true*. Your mother is living here and now, a force in our lives far more truly than she ever was on earth, far better able to help us and love us and look after us. We must live in that knowledge, and in the certainty that she is with us all the time, intensely interested in everything we do and think.

God bless you and keep you and make His face to shine upon you, my dear son.

Your ever loving Daddy.

My Aunt Rachel considers that John and Denys's deaths were in part attributable to the kind of philosophy my grandfather reveals in this letter. In John's case, 'the utmost for the highest' only too literally applies to the manner of his death. And it could be argued, perhaps, that when my father applied to join the anti-tank regiment he was impelled by something of the same attitude, even if my grandfather would have disagreed bitterly with his way of expressing it.

As for me, my grandfather, with his idealism and high-mindedness, reinforced the powerful sense of duty – the duty to achieve great things, preferably for the sake of others – that my absent father had instilled in me. But there were other men around me as I grew up who were of a different hue. My mother remained an active Communist, and many of her political associates became friends of the family. Some of these were intellectuals, but many were working-class activists. In particular, there were the busmen that my mother had recruited into the Party at Holloway bus-garage, where she sold the *Daily Worker* every morning. These men were around our house a lot, and being Communists they too were idealists in their way. But they also had a strong sense of fun and they liked to let their hair down, and there were many evenings of sing-songs and knees-ups and drunkenness at Communist Party 'socials' in the local Co-op Hall and at my mother's parties at the house.

There was also an influence of working-class men from my mother's own family. Her father died when I was still quite young after having his legs amputated, and all I really remember of him is a thin, shrunken figure in the little Gillingham council house, complaining that he could still feel his legs and wanted to scratch them. But there were also the twin brothers, Douglas and Dudley. Like the busmen, these warm-hearted men had an endless supply of teasing humour and a protective cynicism against the vicissitudes of the world. From them I learnt that to be male could involve something altogether less spiritual and more fun than the influence I got from the Hoylands.

Finally there were the lodgers. These, too, came via the Communist Party, and tended to be foreigners. The one I remember most clearly was a Nigerian whose full name – which he patiently taught me – was Onyenkaonyebakaranaiisiohuo-baobudabaobubaraworawari. We however, called him Frank.

It fell to Frank to fulfil one of the more awkward of a father's responsibilities in my life, which was to teach me about the facts of life. While I was in my first year at the boarding school, an older boy developed a crush on me and invited me to go on holiday in the Lake District with him – an invitation which, with my inherited passion for mountains, I was only too eager to comply. So my mother asked Frank to explain the facts of life to me, including the fact of homosexuality, and this he did (to our mutual embarrassment) in the kitchen of our Highgate home.

These various men gave me, by their examples, a certain amount of information about what it meant to be male. But the contact with them tended to be irregular or impermanent, so that in the end my father's non-existence remained a more potent influence on me than these men's existence.

My mother finally married again when I was sixteen, to my great happiness. It was late in life to acquire a father, but I was nevertheless terribly pleased to have one – and I think I owe at least some of my certainties about what matters in life to my stepfather Jack's wise enthusiasms.

When I was twenty-one, I discovered that my father, also, made the attempt to talk to me from beyond the grave.

As well as all those letters he wrote to me from the war, there was another letter. He wrote it before he went to the front and

151

gave it to my mother, to be opened by me when I was twenty-one if he should die. Almost certainly, he did this without knowing that his father had done exactly the same thing for him and his brother John.

I did not even know of this letter's existence until my mother gave it to me at the appointed time. She kept her letters and photos in a small oak writing desk, the kind with a flap that comes down to reveal compartments for envelopes and writing paper and correspondence. The day after my twenty-first birthday, when I was alone with her in the kitchen in our house in Highgate, she told me about the letter, and sat at the writing desk and got it out.

I don't know why – it was, on reflection, stupid of me – but I felt that this letter was something she would want to share with me, and I asked her if she would like to read it to me.

'All right,' she said, and she started. But she had only read two or three words when she burst into tears.

'I can't,' she sobbed. 'John, don't make me, I can't.'

I was shocked at this reminder that she still felt so much grief for my father. Not for the first time, I felt that through my ineptness I had made her grief worse, rather than better.

I took the letter from her, and went shakily upstairs to my room to read it on my own.

In his letter, my father told me that my mother was a wonderful person that I should always appreciate and love, and he said that on the basis of his two years of knowing me, he was sure that I was a wonderful person as well. He said that he hoped I would be brave and kind and strong and that I would be a good elder brother to Bill, and then went on to give me two specific pieces of advice. One of these was Polonius's words to Laertes in *Hamlet*: 'This above all: to thine own self be true, and it must follow, as night the day, thou canst not then be false to any man.'

The other piece of advice – or hope, rather – was that, like him, I would try to devote my life 'to the greatest cause in the world: the emancipation of mankind'. He also said, more simply: 'Have fun and do something useful.'

This much of the letter I remember, but I'm afraid I cannot tell you any more about it, still less quote it in full – because, as you've probably guessed, this precious letter also I have lost.

It grieves me terribly that I have lost it, and many's the time I have ransacked my possessions in the vain hope of finding it. But it's gone – in fact it's been gone these twenty years and more.

I can only think that in some way I wanted to lose these things – that all these reminders of death depressed and disturbed me, and I wanted to cut myself off from them. Now I feel differently about it, but it's too late.

My father was killed on a field in Italy on 13 September 1944.

In 1982 I went to visit his grave.

I was the first member of the family to have done so. My mother could never face it, and no one else in the family was too keen on making the trip either. No one even knew exactly where the cemetery was. My mother told me the English name for the cemetery was Coriano Ridge, and she also gave me some numbers that were supposed to say where the grave was. But what part of Italy it was in, or what the cemetery was called in Italian, she didn't know.

In 1981/2, I spent a year living in central Italy, and while I was there I wrote to the British Embassy in Rome, asking them if they knew where my father's grave was and giving them the few details my mother had told me. I received a letter back from the War Graves Commission, which had a section attached to the Embassy. It told me that the cemetery was near Rimini, gave precise directions for finding it, and said that my father was buried in plot 7, row 5, grave 11.

The Embassy also sent me a leaflet about the battle of Coriano Ridge, saying that it was one of the stiffest battles of the advance through Italy, and that many British and Australian soldiers lost their lives there before the German lines were finally pushed back.

I went to visit the cemetery with a friend on my way back to England. We drove up from Perugia, where I had been staying, in five hours, arriving in the vicinity of the cemetery in the mid-afternoon.

The cemetery's location was a shock to me, because it was only a few hundred yards from the main road between Rimini and Catolica. I had frequently travelled up and down that road when I was nineteen, during a summer spent working in Catolica as a travel courier – passing, without knowing it, within half a mile of my father's mortal remains.

During that summer in 1960, a seventeen-year-old boy staying with the travel company I worked for accidentally gassed himself in a hotel shower heated by a faulty Ascot. I had to go to the hospital to be on hand with the company's chief rep, an energetic Italian woman called Bruna, who drove us there very fast – along that same Catolica-Rimini road – in her little red MG sports-car.

When we got there the boy was on a life support system. The pumping of the oxygen tube down his throat caused his chest to rise and fall as if he was breathing, and we all believed, as we watched him lying there, that he must still be alive. He looked young and beautiful, a sheet thrown over the lower part of his body, his feet protruding from the end, his hairless, sunburnt chest rising and falling, rising and falling. But in fact he had been dead for several hours, and eventually the doctors switched off the machine. I remember thinking how absolutely still he became, and how wrong this seemed, how incomprehensible that he wasn't really there any more, that he had become just a thing. I had never seen somebody die before.

His parents were there as well, completely stupefied. It was Bruna who did all the crying.

I recalled this incident as my friend and I turned off the Catolica-Rimini road and took a narrow lane into the country-side. It was mid-July, and the Italian summer had already sucked the moisture out of most of the landscape, turning it dry and brown. But the cemetery, which we soon came to, was beautifully green. The turf was soft and well-kept, it was shaded by pretty weeping willows, and there was even an English hedge round the periphery, protecting it from the alien aridity outside.

And there were rows and rows of white gravestones.

We located my father's grave without difficulty, counting off the numbers the Embassy had given us. It was a simple grave, like all the others, with just his name, rank and regiment on it (as on the letters he sent me), his age, and the date he was killed. The only thing that distinguished it from the other graves was that most of them had crosses on, whereas my father's didn't. Someone – my mother? – must have informed the War Graves Commission that he was an atheist.

I stood looking down at the grave and tried to make sense of what I was seeing. It was difficult. For all those years, my father had been an abstraction, a non-corporeal entity, a memory – and the fact that he had died in another country had added to his insubstantiality. Now, here I was, standing over what was left of him as a physical being.

He had been so young – much younger than I was now.

How can a father be younger than you are?

'You poor sod,' I found myself thinking, aware that this was perhaps a strange way to address him. 'What a bloody shame. I'm so sorry . . .'

We stayed there for an hour or so. It was a peaceful spot. I sat on the ground in the shade of one of the willow trees. I thought that any minute I would be overwhelmed by intense feelings of grief, but no such feelings came. Instead I found myself almost enjoying the beauty of the place.

Eventually, we walked back to a circular building at the entrance to the cemetery. There was a large open book in it for visitors to make comments. I added a comment of my own, and read some of the others:

'Sam, not a day passes without me thinking of you. I will never forget.'

'It must never happen again.'

I sometimes wonder about the manner of his dying.

Was it quick or slow? Did he know he was going? How bad was the pain?

Did he feel himself sinking, feel himself slipping away? Did he protest, did he try to will himself back?

Did he think of his wife and children at all? Did he think about Communism?

Or was he in no fit state to think about anything. Was he so engulfed in pain, did the pain propel him so pitilessly towards his extinction, that his mind was only filled with a sense of horror too great for the living to imagine . . .

Or was it all over too quickly for this. Just an explosion somewhere in his body and a brief 'Oh fuck' and then nothing.

I don't even know if he swore. Probably not – son of a Quaker etc. But then again, maybe.

I have always believed that he died bravely – that in complete disgregard for his own safety etc, he went to rescue one of his men who was wounded, and that he was killed trying to pull the man back. But I'm not sure where I got this idea from, or if this is what really happened. I don't know if he was machine-gunned, or mortared, or what.

His commanding officer wrote to my mother after he died, and said that Denys was an outstanding officer who was loved by his men.

A year ago I went to Hove to tape-record an interview with my mother. I wanted to know about her life before I was born, and I wanted to know more about my father. Over the years I had accumulated many details and impressions about him, but there was still a lot I didn't know.

My mother had been a little reluctant to do this at first, but in the event she answered all my questions. She talked to me for over three hours, telling me many, many things I had not known before.

I realised, as she talked, that it had always been difficult for me to feel straightforward feelings of love for my father, even though I had worshipped him and his memory as a child. He had made my mother bitterly unhappy by dying, and his death had also cast a long shadow over my own life. Inevitably, I had thought of him as someone who caused unhappiness, no matter how unwittingly.

But now my mother told me how he had made her happy – how she had been happy throughout those interrupted years she knew him. And she gave me a new sense of him as a person – a person who was great to be with, a person who made friends with everybody, a person who loved wild flowers, a person who wore bright red trousers when he was walking down a country lane.

She talked about him as a lover and a friend, and she talked about his death with sadness, but without that anger that had so often devastated me as a child.

I found myself experiencing a sense of love for him that I had scarcely ever been able to feel before.

When we had finished, she said:

'I know I should have told you all this long ago. Your Grandad always used to tell me I ought to tell you as much as I could about Denys. He said that after his mother died when he was small, his father made a point of telling him and his brother as much as he could about her. And when his wife Helen died, he told Denys and John as much as he could about her. He felt it was important that they should know, and he said I should do the same about Denys to you. But I couldn't do it. Whenever I tried, I broke down . . .'

She paused, and then added:

'Did you know that your Grandad's father was married for five years before his wife died, leaving two small sons? And your Grandad was married for five years before his wife died, leaving two small sons? And that Denys and I were married for five years before he died, leaving two small sons? . . . Isn't that strange.'

Before I left the house, we went to her writing desk in the dining-room – still the same writing desk she had had in Highgate – and she got out all those old photos of Denys again. All those photos of my Dad.

It was then that I broke up inside. He had such a lovely face, he had such a lovely grin, he seemed such a lovely man, I could not bear it.

I managed somehow to say goodbye to my mother, stumbled out of the house, and walked down the quiet streets of Hove to the station.

I cried for most of the journey back to London.

AN ORDINARY WIZARD

PAUL ATKINSON

My mother left my father ten years ago or so. I was twenty-eight. It was to be a temporary separation, but my father was terrified. I sat with him one night in their kitchen. He couldn't bear to be anywhere else in the house. The empty rooms tortured him with her absence. It was no longer a home for him, he said. He couldn't sleep. We sat all night. He was huddled up inside his coat, shaking, and telling me how frightened he was. I felt frightened too. I sat and held his hand, listening to his fear, knowing there was nothing I could say that would make any real difference.

I remembered an earlier occasion when I sat with my father, caught up in my mother's absence. It was in a different house, a smaller, terraced house in which my mother had been born. It was our family home until I was sixteen. I sat with my father and my two younger brothers. It was a Friday night. I was eight or so. For a while, my parents had an arrangement. On Fridays, my mother had a night out. She got dressed up, put on her deep red lipstick and went dancing at the Palais with her friends. My father went out on Saturdays to the Conservative Club to play snooker and drink with his brother-in-law. We sat up together, waiting for my mother to return. My father was reading the evening paper while we watched the TV. I was clean and damp in my pyjamas after a bath in front of the fire.

It was late, late enough for the Continental Movie. I caught a glimpse of a naked breast above the subtitles and felt embarrassed. Could he tell that I was interested? Was he interested? What was happening inside him? We were waiting, in silence. I knew we should be in bed, and felt uncomfortable. I watched the tight muscles in his jaw as he ate. He hated her going out without him. Everything was out of place. What was she doing? Who was she with? He was in the grip of a possessive rage. We sat and kept vigil.

For much of the time during the early years of my childhood, my mother and father seemed trapped in an irreconcilable conflict, like two turbulent rivers wrestling in a confined channel – wild waters unwilling to mix. They argued constantly – about money, about housework, about looking after the three of us, about going out, about anything. My mother seemed perpetually unhappy, driven by a demon I didn't understand. She nagged and badgered him with a numbing violence. Her unhappiness hung in the air, a backcloth against which everything took place.

At times, the house was filled with a terrible tension. It hung in the air, almost suffocating. It paralysed movement, contaminated the food. There was no escape. At night I lay in bed with my brothers, listening in the dark to the angry voices. Frightened and sad, I would rock myself to sleep.

My father would usually bend to my mother's fury. He seemed able to manoeuvre within its cramped space, sometimes deflecting, sometimes absorbing. Occasionally he could bear no more. An explosion of boiling rage would burst out of him and blast through the house. I remember one Sunday afternoon after dinner I watched the argument mount. My brothers and I sat in the front room on the studio-couch in frozen silence as my father cleared the table. My mother was in the kitchen doing the pots. She was shouting at him, about what I don't know. Perhaps it was this house, where she'd lived all her life. She hated it, and all the memories it held. Her shouting became wild and hysterical. I could see him boiling up inside. His body stiffened with rage. He was carrying the table back into the kitchen. Suddenly, he exploded, hurling the table across the room. With a tremendous crash, it hit the back door, smashing the door panels out into the yard outside.

For a moment everything stopped. I was terrified. The worst seemed to have happened. And then my mother laughed. I couldn't believe it. With one mighty thunderbolt, the storm had passed. The air was clear and I could breathe. My father started to gather up the broken door. My mother carried on with the pots. I wanted to laugh with relief.

If my father had stood up to my mother's biting unhappiness more often, perhaps those early years would have been different. Who knows? As it was, I took my mother's side, and allied myself with her misery. He seemed hard and cold to me. I felt he really was refusing to give her something, something that would make her happy.

He seemed a long way away. He was out at work, of course. He was an electrician. His apprenticeship had been interrupted by the war and completed in the navy as an electrician/torpedo-man. He sailed around the world twice and never saw action. Then he worked for firms for a few years, teaching his trade to his own apprentices. Not long after I was born, he set up as self-employed. He couldn't bear being under another man's control. In the summer, sitting out in the sun on the street in front of the house, I watched him ride by on his black bike, steel tubing tied to the crossbar and a toolbag across his back.

In the house, my father carried about him the mystery of another world. In the morning, he had gone before my day started. In the evening, he arrived like a stranger from an alien land. His body moved in an unfamiliar rhythm, carrying home the world outside. He smelt of somewhere else.

They were smells that I associated with his workshop in the attic. A steep staircase climbed up out of our bedroom on to a cold, concrete floor which was lit from above by a skylight. What a room! It had a huge, wooden bench scarred and oily, with a rusty vice bolted to one corner; dozens of tools scattered everywhere or hanging in racks, made of dark metal with worn wooden handles; saws and files with rasping edges, hammers and wrenches too heavy to lift; ancient soldering irons, cans of grease, boxes and boxes of screws, bolts, wooden rawl-plugs, electrical fittings; drums of cables in black, green and red. It was a room filled with danger and excitement, filled with my father and the artefacts of his magical trade. Standing in it, I felt tiny and awed, my imagination bursting with my father's wizardry. Yet I never saw him in this magician's tower. The workshop was always deserted. My father practised elsewhere.

In the conflict between my parents, my father's foreignness became malign. Perhaps as first born I fostered a special claim to my mother – against him and my brothers. It was a secret claim. I was locked away inside myself most of the time. I brooded in a rather lonely, unhappy world of my own. I was caught up with my mother's depression, I think. I wanted to make her feel happy. I suppose I wanted her to be happy so she would make me feel happy. At night, in bed, I entered a recurring fantasy. On the street, a beautiful woman is in terrible danger. She has fallen into the road in front of a bus, perhaps. I leap out to save her, to push her out of the way, and am injured in the process. The wound is deep and poignant. As I lie in hospital, close to death but never dying, the woman comes to nurse me.

Bathed in the sublime glow of a dying hero, I would slip off to sleep.

No one knew about this private world. I didn't want them to. Years later, as an adult visiting my parents, my father and I sat up late, talking. 'We couldn't really make you out, you know', he said. 'You seemed to be in a world of your own. But you seemed to be all right, so we left you to it.'

As I got older, the conflict in the house continued. It was like living in a pressure cooker, all cooped up together, trying to survive the daily round. But something was changing. My father took shape as a person. I became more actively involved in the tension and fighting. In the mornings, he was around as we got ready for school. He would push and cajole us through breakfast, getting washed and cleaning our shoes. I would sometimes resist him, answering him back or occasionally flaring up in anger. His reaction to open defiance was terrifying. But it was better than cowering inside.

In the evenings, or over the weekend, my brothers and I would often become targets for his smouldering anger. You could feel it building up inside him, moving inevitably towards explosion. As it built up, I would begin to tense up inside, until it became almost impossible to move. Anything could ignite the explosive fumes in the air. And yet the desire to light the touch-paper was overwhelming. A moment of defiance or open resentment, finding its cue with immaculate timing in a score I could no longer resist, and my father's rage broke over me like a tidal wave. He would fly at me with his fists, spitting with rage. Mesmerised for a moment, I'd watch the blood-vessels bulging in his face, before curling up in a corner to fend off the blows. Sometimes I ran, fleeing upstairs with him crashing behind in wild pursuit. Afterwards, I would retreat inward to the deepest, most inaccessible place, where I could hide with my cargo of hatred and bitterness, confirmed in heroism and suffering. And yet it was also a relief. For a while the tension was gone, and perhaps a different contact would follow – something more open, perhaps a little sad. There was an unspoken reconciliation as life was allowed to resume.

When all three of us – my brothers and I – were in trouble, it wasn't so bad. In fact, it was almost fun. At night, we would play in bed together, shouting and fighting, pushing each other out on to the floor. My father would keep coming upstairs, getting more and more angry. Once he went wild, bashing us around the room. 'I'll get you up with me in the morning. You keep me up all night, I'll get you up early.' And he did. We shivered and mooched in a cold front room, miserable and silent in the dead light of dawn. But it ruined his quiet, first hour alone in the house and he never tried that one again.

And there were some good moments now, moments of joy even. Did good and bad run alongside each other without properly meeting? Or perhaps we were just beginning to relate more. My brothers and I would set on him on the front room carpet, pinning him down, wrestling amid the furniture, the restrictions of my mother's orderliness temporarily cast aside. It was wonderful to feel the strength of his body, to pit myself against him. The three of us, for a delightful moment, held him in our power, tickling, rubbing his ears, bending back a thumb, shrieking with the excitement and effort of matching his hard muscles.

There was the chance, under cover of play, to vent a quota of sadistic revenge. I would really try to hurt him. Once, in the middle of a fight, I wrenched back a finger with all my might. He howled in pain and threw us all off. The game was over. 'If you've stopped me going to work tomorrow, I'll kill you.' I felt guilty. I knew for me the fun was mixed with hatred. I'd destroyed a good moment.

In the backyard, we played cricket together. The wicket was chalked up on the coal-house wall. He liked to bowl, setting out his field as best he could in the tiny yard. What delight when the ball hit a window, or went sailing into a neighbour's yard, or better still over the back wall into the forbidden world of the football ground whose main stand overshadowed the back of the house. My father became a delinquent Zeus, a mischievous older brother leading us into trouble. It was a joy to be one of his gang.

He bought a van as business improved. It was crimson and black, with a pointed nose and flaring mudguards. The back had windows in it, and he fitted a bench seat for us. The van sat outside the house, a bright red stallion, a bringer of adventure and power. We drove out to Derbyshire for the day, everyone in their place. My father was behind the wheel, my mother beside him, we three bubbling with excitement behind. Returning home, there was a moment of special peace, curled up exhausted alongside my brothers, deliciously safe in my parents' hands as we hummed through the strange land of night. In the van, I could escape for a while from the shadows and conflicts of home.

I was shy of any special attention, especially from my father, though in truth I wanted it enough. My brothers were freer than me, I think – though perhaps they wouldn't agree. Here too, I was caught up in a fantasy of my own: that it was my job to keep the peace, to mediate between them and my parents. This was the burden of my special place. I separated myself and stood aloof from both camps. When my father converted his workshop into a bedroom for my brothers, I slept alone in the small room we had shared, and listened to them playing around in bed. Still frightened of the tension and anger downstairs, I was caught between the two worlds of my parents and my younger brothers.

Sleeping alone in that room scared me. The floodlights of the football ground next door lit up my curtain and made monsters in its folds. Once, in a fit of terror, I shouted and screamed, bringing my father up to me. Gently, he reassured me there was nothing there and moved the curtain open for me to see. It was a moment of great tenderness and warmth. I felt his concern for me. Perhaps for the first time, I felt loved by him. I fell asleep in his warmth and the curtain-monsters lost their power.

When I was eight or nine, he built me a pigeon loft. I had talked

167

about wanting to keep pigeons, like some of the other kids in the street. I was amazed when he announced he would build me a loft. It was just for me. I couldn't quite take it in. He worked on it all weekend with great care and skill. Its inner wall, a frame of chicken wire, lifted out to let me close to the birds and to clean out its floor. It had an entrance of bobs which could be locked, and a sliding side door to release them for flight. I kept a beautiful pair of pigeons. I fed them and watered them, and cleaned out their loft. I watched them breed, helped them rear their chicks, called them in from the roofs when I came home from school. Once, I took them to school. I stood in front of the class with a bird in my hand, talking about how to keep them. I loved them, and it was a love which I associated with my father and the loft he had built for me.

Then, when I was twelve or thirteen, my relationship with my father was transformed. He asked me one evening if I'd like to come out to work with him during school holidays. I said yes, and entered his other world.

Early one morning, while the rest of the house was sound asleep, I joined my father in what until now had been a private ritual. This had been my father's time alone with the house, while everyone else was still dreaming – now it was mine, too. It was a quiet, unhurried time. He made his first cup of tea and smoked a first cigarette. Outside, with the cold half-light of dawn, the street began to awake. My father, too, slowly came to life. He made a packed lunch and a flask of tea, thinking aloud about what materials he needed to take for the day's work. Would we need to visit the wholesaler first? He was talking to himself. This new world had its own language, as yet mysterious to me.

I knew I was in the grip of a momentous change. I was to be part of my father's foreign world, which I had only seen as an outsider. Already, that first morning, I was with a different side of him, and it brought out a different side of me. I was now his work-mate, as well as his son. In this other world, he was a teacher. I was his apprentice. It was not simply a trade he had to teach. His work was also an outlook on life. It was woven into his identity. It rooted him in the world around him. His work gave him a sense of pride and self-respect. Working alongside him, I got to know him in a new way.

Our first job together was in a part of Nottingham I had never seen before. It was a huge, empty Victorian house – three or four times the size of our home. We had called in at the wholesaler's on the way. My father talked to a fat, balding man in a silk waistcoat who was smoking a cigar. When my father introduced me as his son, I said hello with a shy pride. My world was expanding at an alarming rate.

The house needed a complete rewire. It was daunting. I felt so awkward and inept. I didn't know anything. The tools, so familiar to my father, were mysterious to me. I didn't even know their names. And it wasn't just the work itself. I had never spent so much time with my father. I didn't really know how to be with him, how to talk. Nor did he. We were having to learn together.

It was winter. The house was freezing. He showed me how to use the hand-brace and asked me drill holes in a row of joists for the cables to run through. It was awful. I couldn't use the brace. I didn't have the strength or the skill. I was desperate to make a good start, but the cold and enormity of the task overwhelmed me. Each hole was torture. In the end, I was close to tears. I said his job looked easier than mine. He immediately offered to exchange jobs. 'I always used to say to my lads, when they thought I was making them do the dirty work, "OK, let's swap jobs. That's fine." ' So we exchanged. Of course, his turned out to be much harder than mine.

Each day he taught me to use his tools. Step by step, as the need

169

arose, he taught the theory and practice of his trade. Like a master craftsman, he worked with a sureness of skill and a quiet, unspoken pride. Each aspect of the work – whether running out cables under floorboards, or putting up steel trunking, whether chasing and replastering walls, or making the final fixings and connections – each had its secrets, its problems, and its art. Each could be done well or badly. He handled each operation, each tool, with the dexterity and confidence of use.

He made it seem so easy. He is a big, deep-chested man. I watched his grey-blue eyes, deep-set under a thick bush of brow, as he concentrated on what he was doing. He managed to chain-smoke, whatever he was doing with his hands. His fingers were long and elegant, but so strong and sure. I felt awkward beside him. I thought I'd never be any good at it. As I struggled with a hammer and chisel, or tried to fish out a cable from under the floorboards, he would get exasperated. 'God, you're like a bloody woman. Get out of the way.' And I would stand aside, feeling humiliated and wretched.

For the first week or so, we hardly spoke, except for him to tell me what to do, or me to ask him again how to do it. When I didn't understand, I'd pretend I did, in case he lost his temper. 'No, not like that. Here! Like this!' It was a probationary period, I suppose. He didn't know any more than I did whether it was going to work.

Gradually, it did work. We came home one evening and my mother asked how it was going. 'OK!', said my dad. 'He's getting the hang of it.' It was music to my ears. After a couple of months, I knew it was going to be all right. We were both relaxing. One day, working alongside another tradesman, I was introduced. 'Ah, so this is your son. Following in your father's footsteps, eh?' My father cut in. 'Oh, I don't think he'll be carrying tools when he leaves school' – I was at grammar school – 'but he's good at it.

He could be an electrician if he wanted to be.' My heart soared. I heard the pride in his voice and was overjoyed.

Now, as we worked together and drove home in the evenings, he began to tell me the stories of his youth. He talked about his own apprenticeship, how he was treated by tradesmen and employers. He told stories of the men he liked and trusted, who were open and fair, and told of his contempt for abuse and injustice. He told me about the places he'd worked, about the Jewish factory owners up in the lace market, about the workshops out in the Derbyshire hills where he'd had to be 'billeted' with local families. His stories were filled with a mixture of bitterness and humour.

He talked about the pettiness and greed of the family firm he had worked for – the arrogant boss's son who treated the men with contempt and found endless excuses to dock their pay. He told about the scrapes he and his mates got into, and the jokes they played on each other. There were men he respected, some he despised. Of others, he told with compassion their stories of misfortune and inadequacy. This world of his apprenticeship and early years at work lived in him as if it were yesterday.

The more we worked together, travelling around Nottingham and out into the East Midlands, the more my confidence grew. And with it, the relationship with my father. No longer worried about failing, I relaxed with him, and began to see much more of the person he was. We were working in Leicester on a series of petrol stations. They were big jobs. A dozen or more other men worked alongside us – mainly labourers. Our boss was a millionaire, who arrived in his Rolls now and again. Working alongside all these other men, my father was thrown into relief.

I realised he was a shy, rather self-possessed man. He kept himself almost aloof. It wasn't that he was unfriendly. On the contrary, he got along with everyone. He had a tremendous sense of fairness, and as far as I could tell was respected by everyone we met. But he was rather uncomfortable with these men. Though he joined in, I could tell that he was awkward with the banter and piss-take. He seemed on edge, almost humiliated at times. At first, I thought he was better than them. They were too rough, rather common. As a tradesman, he was an 'aristocrat of labour'. Perhaps we were rather superior. But I could sense his fear of them and it shocked me. As I got to know the other men a little, I realised it was something in him that held back. There was a brittleness about him. It was as if he felt inferior or inadequate in some way, and that he was going to be attacked.

It found expression as an issue of class. Many of his stories about his employers, and his officers in the Navy, burned with an acid contempt I couldn't really understand. There was the employer who had sent him to work in Derbyshire. The client there had booked him into the local hotel. The usual practice was to find digs with a village family. After a week's work, he arrived back at his employers to get his wages, and was told that the hotel bill was coming out of his wage packet and there was nothing left. It was a misunderstanding, I suppose. The client eventually cleared it up, and paid the hotel bill as he had always intended. But in my father's telling, maybe twenty-five years later, there was not only anger and a sense of injustice. There was a murderous hatred, humiliation and a thirst for revenge still burning inside. That moment, standing in the office of a hard-nosed employer refusing to pay him, consumed him each time the story was told.

He talked about class a lot, always with passion. His instincts were socialist and egalitarian. In his relationships with people, he seemed to practice what he believed. I never saw him put people down. On the few occasions he talked about the men we were working with, he startled me with the acuteness of his insight. This perceptiveness about people was something he kept close to his chest. And yet his passion for fairness and equality rang false, too. Its vehemence was driven by his own sense of inferiority, which gnawed away inside him and which he could never admit. I could see it when we met someone middle class. Anyone who dressed in middle-class clothes, or spoke with a middle-class accent, or held himself in a middle-class manner was likely to knock my father off balance. He would so often go on the defensive. 'I'm as good as any man. These people pretend to be something they're not. He thinks he's better than an ordinary working man.'

I couldn't make sense of this passion in him at the time. I could identify with his humiliation and anger, but its source and meaning puzzled me. I wanted him to be unassailable, reassuringly capable. At the same time, it gave me a window into my father as a person. His vulnerability made him more like me. Later, when I went to university and felt so overwhelmed and insignificant in a middle-class, southern world, I turned to class to express my anger and feelings of inferiority. It was not until my late twenties that I could begin to see how much like my father I am.

How my father was at home became clearer, too. Again there was a mixture of discomfort and warmth as he let me see who he was. Driving home from a job out of town, tired and relaxed, we would occasionally talk about the family. These were conversations which began to heal some of the splits inside me. I noticed, when we were with the other men and the conversation turned to women, my father became silent. Of course, my presence inhibited him. But that was only part of the picture. When he did speak of my mother, it was with respect rather than anger or blame. But the tension with her came through. He said that she was to be handled with care. There was initiation in his voice.

And perhaps a plea for understanding. 'She's irrational, really. There's no good arguing with her past a certain point. I can't explain to her about money or what has to be done to keep work going. She thinks I can spend as much time at home as I please, or take time off when I want.' It was as if she were alien, a different species.

He knew she was unhappy and that there was too much fighting at home. He told me about her childhood, how awful it had been. They were stories I had already heard, but they carried a different meaning now. She was from a much poorer background than he was. Her father had been a bigamist. When my mother was young, her father was spotted in the streets of Nottingham by his first wife's brother. So he abandoned the family, telling no one what was happening, and was never seen again. My mother's older sister died of pneumonia at eleven. Her brother, William, spent his teens in borstal, married the borstal cook who was twice his age, and joined the RAF. He was killed in the early months of the war in a flying accident in India. My mother, surrounded by death and abandonment, was left to look after her own embittered mother.

When they married, my father moved in with my mother – into a house which, for my mother, held so much pain and loss. This was the same house I grew up in. Her mother died soon after. She fell one winter, crossing the icy yard to the lavatory. My mother blamed my father. He had refused to help his mother-in-law over the icy yard. Throughout my childhood, she campaigned bitterly to get out of that house and leave its pain behind. Occasionally she spoke of the deaths of her brother and her sister, always with inconsolable pain. Somewhere in her, I think, she expected my father, too, to leave her and her children to die.

I heard my father's story, too, as we drove between Leicester and Nottingham. He was the youngest of four, the only son. His father had been illegitimate and abandoned by his parents. He lost a leg after a football accident, and died young of drink. My father's mother was the only grandparent I knew. She died recently. We found her – my father, my son and I – lying on the kitchen floor of her council flat. I visited her later in hospital and held her frail, wrinkled hand. It was the first and last time she and my son met. She had always seemed distant and hard to me. As a child I visited her with my father on Sundays. She was sixty when I was seven. The visits were formal. She lived in the world of her past. She cleaned her home constantly; the dark sideboard and lace antimacassars, the hearth, her stuffed sofa, a copper in the scullery, old photographs in a cold parlour which was never used. She gave us liquorice allsorts. My brothers and I sat quiet and awed in our Sunday suits. She was never still. She made tea, carried on cleaning, humping in the coal, moving things about. She had been in domestic service most of her life. After a few minutes, my father sat and read the paper. They had nothing to say to each other. We all sat silent, familiar yet strange.

When he spoke of his mother, it was with the same distant respect that he spoke of his wife. She had had a hard life, and brought up four kids alone. 'She's fiercely independent, you know. She had a real reputation for being tough, putting up with nothing. God, she could be hard.' He was speaking with affection. I thought she was cold, even cruel.

Meanwhile, at home, my mother had also begun to take me into her confidence. She told me her grievances against my father. He was tight with money, wouldn't tell her how much he was making or had in the bank. He wouldn't take her out, go dancing or socialise. He didn't like her to have friends, didn't want people visiting the house. He was cold emotionally, wouldn't share his feelings with her, wouldn't let her in. And she talked about sex. She told me he was inhibited and shy and didn't meet her sexually.

I felt angry and torn at being drawn into her confidence. I wanted it, yet felt excruciatingly uncomfortable. Deep longings and conflicts were stirred. Was I to be her alternative lover, with whom she could share her feelings and needs? Was she treating me as the daughter she had always wanted? She lived with four men. But, as she watched me enter my father's world, I think her fear of losing me became acute.

In a sense, she was right. Working with my father helped release me from my childhood. His cooler, more observed take on the conflict with my mother encouraged me to distance myself from it. I had a sense for the first time that it was really not my problem. I could be angry with my mother without having to take sides. I could feel close to my father without betraying her. They were two separate people, and their relationship with each other was their concern, not mine.

At last, I began to come out of myself. I felt a new sense of freedom from the family. I spent less time with my brothers, less time out on the streets, which, as a child, had been my escape from the enclosed space of home. My friendships at grammar school became more important. I began to play guitar. I started on a home-made construction of wood and cardboard. I was amazed and delighted when my parents bought me a proper guitar for my birthday. At school, friends and I formed a rhythm and blues band, and for a while played small gigs in pubs and a couple of school dances. My father drove us around Nottingham with the mess of our equipment in the back of his van, enjoying our company and the excitement of performance.

At this point, for a year or two, my father and I were closer than we had ever been. Our lives overlapped. Working together, I felt increasingly like a partner. If not quite an equal, I would share in the planning of a job, take some initiatives, ask his advice rather than be shown how to do it. Driving around with the band, my friends and I let him into our group. He shared our friendship, some of the madness of adolescence. There was, for a moment, a delightful mutuality.

But the seeds of a separation were already sown. At the local grammar school, I was already on foreign soil. My father placed a high premium on education. He worked hard at getting all three of us the best schooling he could. I was more academic than my younger brothers. After I passed the Eleven-plus, he encouraged me to do homework in the evening and visited the school on open days. But otherwise I was left to get on with it. My father was uncomfortable with the middle-class ethos of the school. When he met my teachers, I could feel the struggle going on inside him. As a boy, he had won a scholarship himself, but the family hadn't the money to send him.

As I became immersed in Latin and Greek texts, I was sailing in uncharted waters. My father must have felt a mixture of pride and envy. At first, I felt alien and lost myself. But, gradually, there was excitement, as the horizon began to roll back and open out on to a new world. Among my friends on the street, I was the only one who got into grammar school. I visited the houses of my grammar school friends and felt ashamed of mine – ashamed of my mother and father, too. The conflict of feelings was almost unbearable – self-hatred and shame, contempt for my parents, and anger at my friends and their families. Now, I enjoy the irony of my own son, at fourteen, feeling ashamed to be on the streets with me, his middle-class father, in case he is spotted by his pals from his inner London comprehensive.

Meanwhile, another force was brewing which was to drive a wedge between me and my father, and bring an abrupt end to this period of closeness: sex!

In that tiny house, the five of us were squashed up on top of each other. Life had a powerful biological undertow. There was no privacy. For the first few years, my brothers and I shared a bed. There was a chamber pot under the bed that was used every night. The whole family took it in turns to wash in the kitchen and take a bath in the front room in front of the fire. My parents' bodies, the dark, mysterious flavour of their sexuality, fascinated and appalled me. Their bedroom held their secrets. Occasionally the noises of their love-making came to me through the wall at night and disturbed me with dark fantasies. Sometimes we went in there to play games like hide and seek, or to dive off the wardrobe on to their bed. I could smell their bodies among the sheets, my mother's clothes and make-up, the drawers of underwear, the basket of dirty clothes.

Evidence of my mother's body seemed to be everywhere. She complained frequently of constipation and had to be on the toilet at a certain time each morning. To be in there when she wanted to use it was a crime. Sanitary towels, wrapped in newspaper, were left in odd places in the house. She was constantly worried about getting fat and told us how much she had and hadn't eaten each day. I regularly bumped into her undressed or half-dressed, and would scan her nakedness spellbound and embarrassed.

By comparison, my father was physically contained and enigmatic. I caught an occasional glimpse of him naked. His dark, hanging genitals filled me with awe. Unlike my mother, he never talked about his body. His references to sex were rare, couched in shy humour. He joked about women queueing ten-deep outside the house, waiting to catch him alone. There were moments of intense concentration on the chorus girls on the TV and an enduring passion for Shirley Bassey.

My own sexuality took shape in fantasy and masturbation and became intimately caught up in the secret longings of my childhood. Once, my mother came into the room as I was masturbating. She said nothing and went back downstairs. In a sweat of fear I heard her ask my father if he thought he should go up and talk to me. 'No', he said, sounding as if he felt something of the same horror I was feeling. I was enormously relieved.

Early games of kissing with the girls on the street – having girlfriends without really knowing why and what to do with them – gradually gave way to more serious stuff. Sexual longing became passionate and urgent, and with it a longing for intimacy. I wanted to share my private world with someone. I wanted someone to want me.

At sixteen, in the sixth form, I met Irene. She lived near our new house and we travelled home together. She was an only child. Her parents were from Lancashire and ran a grocery shop. I began to spend time at Irene's after school, before her parents got home. We talked, and listened to the Rolling Stones. Her mother was strong and warm. Irene had a bright, rebellious self-confidence. We made love on her bed after school. I began to spend as much time as I could with her, and my parents became increasingly angry. Irene very rarely visited my house. I didn't want her to.

As the relationship developed, the school complained that it was too serious and that I would be distracted from my A-levels. Irene was seen as a rather frivolous and empty-headed young woman, disrespectful of authority. My father went to see the headmaster. He came back saying that the school thought it was a sexual infatuation and it seemed to be taking me over. He told me he agreed. I felt betrayed and confused. I couldn't talk about Irene with him. He couldn't talk to me, either. We had never spoken in any open way about relationships with women. We had never talked about sex. My father was as appalled as me that the whole subject, so private and vulnerable, should be exposed to public gaze. He found the meeting with my headmaster excruciating, I'm sure. I certainly couldn't bear to feel anything other than anger and defiance – for both my school and him. In a sense, the school was right. I was overwhelmed by the relationship with Irene. It touched me in that powerful place of unfulfilled longing. It had a momentum of its own, over which I had little control. For my father, I was being led off somewhere dangerous, into the seductive mysteries of the feminine. I was!

During my final year at grammar school, open warfare broke out between my father and me. We rowed constantly over my being at Irene's. Our closeness vanished. I was no longer working with him or playing in the band. I didn't go on the family holidays. I was hardly at home. The only contact I had with him was embattled. He became an ogre again. Perhaps we were in a replay of my earlier struggle to ally with my mother against him. In the final summer, I did become closer to my mother again. She got me a job doing clerical work with her for a few months.

My father seemed determined to win the battle of wills between us. He turned me out of the house a couple of times. I spent a night at Irene's. He threatened to stop me going to university. I had a grant and the offer of places. I didn't see how he could. I had never fought him openly like this. I suppose we were both coming to terms with the fact that I was actually going to leave and go on my own way. I was the eldest. It was new ground for both of us.

The more violently we fought, the less it was just about Irene. I was fighting to get free. There seemed no other way to do it. It had to be a battle. In the end, I left to start a degree course two hundred miles away in the south, full of anger and determined never to go back.

In fact, the drama over my relationship with Irene was not yet ended. Without discussing the implications, we had chosen different universities. While I went south, Irene went north. Perhaps we sensed that we were going to part, that our lives were going in different directions. During the first term at Canterbury,

I struggled with the shock of leaving home and finding myself, without bearings, on a college campus. Irene and I visited each other. For a while, I hated Kent with its predominantly southern, public school students. Irene, I could tell, felt antagonistic to the place. I decided to leave and re-apply to her university.

Almost immediately, things changed. I became friends with a group of people living in hall, and started a sexual relationship with one of the women. After a month or two of confusion and emotional unheaval, I decided to stay at Kent and end with Irene. I went up to see her and after a passionate weekend we parted. Six months later, Irene turned up in Canterbury to tell me that she was pregnant. She had told no one. She thought we could make a go of it and wanted to know what I felt. I felt the bottom had dropped out of my world.

I travelled up to Nottingham in a dream-like state. I remember crossing London on the tube, groaning and mumbling to myself, hardly able to breathe. I was frightened of meeting my father. It was a nightmare. I thought I had left my life in Nottingham behind. I thought the pain and the humiliation of those last few months at home was over. It was now a year since I'd left. My new life at Kent had begun to take off. The disorientation, the loneliness and misery had given way to mounting excitement, a growing sense of expansion and potential. Now I was being dragged backwards. I didn't know what was in store for me, but I felt I had little power over what was going to happen. Between Irene and her family, and my father, vindicated in his opposition to our infatuation, I felt I was about to put my head into the lion's mouth.

I misjudged my father completely. When I arrived home, he had already been in touch with Irene's parents. He asked me if I wanted to marry her. I said no. It was the last thing I wanted. 'OK. So, we'll have to take if from there.' And we did. I met Irene

181

at her parents' house. Facing her mother was awful. There was nothing much to say. Irene had decided she wanted to keep the baby, take a year off college, and try to manage as a single parent. She didn't ask anything of me. In the event, the baby was adopted. I never saw him.

Throughout this crisis of mine, my father supported me as best he could. He gave me an absolute right to choose what I wanted to do. He made no attempt to change my mind. At one point, he said to me, 'You know, this will ruin that girl's life.' I almost died of remorse and shame. But there was a determination in me to just go through it, whatever was necessary, and get back to my new life. And I think my father felt the same. It was a sort of end-game between us. The fight was over. I *had* really left home. I *was* really out in a new world of my own. I would not be living in my parents' world. I was never going to return to Nottingham to live.

When it was all over, when what had to be faced was faced, and the decisions had been made, I left to go back to Canterbury still in a dream-like state. I said nothing particular to my father. I didn't really know what I was feeling. Somewhere inside me, though, I was enormously grateful. The year before I had left in a storm. It was as if our earlier contact had been destroyed. Now, I was leaving with the contact restored, though transformed by an acknowledgment that our relationship had changed. What I chose to do with my life was now up to me.

Exactly ten years later, my mother left my father, and he broke down. That night, sitting with him in the kitchen and watching him enter a terrible nightmare, another boundary-stone was planted in my own life. In the intervening decade, a different story of my relationship with my father had begun to emerge, a story I am probably as yet unable to write. It might begin with a powerful rejection of my childhood, and with it, any identification with my father. I would have to enter the realm of ideas, the ideologies of my twenties, through which I began to look for myself. I would have to talk about the birth of my own son and my own experience of fatherhood. Most of all, I would have to speak of how my father lives inside me, so interwoven with who I am.

I sat with him in the kitchen, that night. Raw terror, wave upon wave, erupted from inside him. The person I normally spoke to was overwhelmed, blinked out, and disappeared. In his place was a terrified child, abandoned and in hell. And it was a child I knew well in myself. I did my best to stay alongside him and discovered I had drawn up alongside myself. Just two human beings, sitting alongside each other. Just two ordinary people, struggling with life. Like it always had been, and would continue to be. Just two human beings, who happened to be father and son.

A TASTE OF SALT

FRANCIS KING

In the course of my life I have had four fathers; but it is of my first and natural father that now, in my sixties, I think most often and most deeply. This puzzles me since, of all my fathers, he is the one to whom I felt least close, whom I never fully understood and who, I am as much convinced now as when he was alive, never fully understood me.

Sometimes, when I am thinking of him with a particular intensity – usually during one of those stretches which each night disrupt my sleep like jagged reefs intermittently impeding the passage of a ship across an otherwise tranquil lagoon – I taste a brine-like salt on my lips. It is literally the taste of him, as I knew it all those years ago in my country of birth, Switzerland, in my country of childhood residence, India, and in my country of education, England. 'Kiss your father goodnight,' my mother would tell me; and with a leaden reluctance I used to cross over to the chair in which he would be reading or doing a crossword and place my lips on his forehead. I would taste that salt. He would never kiss me in return; he would merely respond by putting an arm round my shoulder or by patting me on the back. 'Goodnight, boy,' he would sometimes say; but more often he would say nothing.

Since he was not merely a confident rider but also a daring polo-player, I cannot remember a time when he did not own at least one horse. He would hold out a hand, palm upwards, to one of these horses or to the pony which he had bought for me in the hope, fruitless as it turned out, that I should eventually acquire his own equestrian skill. The animal would then at once begin to lick

187

his palm, its tongue scraping like emergy paper over flesh unnaturally red. But when, with some trepidation, I held out my own hand, not even the pony, ridden by me every day, showed any interest. 'It's the salt,' my father explained. 'My hands are salt, yours are not.'

That salt, I eventually realised, like the flush not merely of his palms but also of his cheeks, was a symptom of his illness. Although my father's body was so strong, wiry and hard, he was nonetheless slowly dying of tuberculosis. It was this which had taken him from India to Switzerland in the hope of a cure, with the result that I was born there, in a hotel in Adelboden; and it was this which presented one obstacle after another – surmounted (as I now see) with exemplary courage – to a career first in the Indian Police and then in the Intelligence Bureau, of which he was Deputy Director at the time of his death.

That was a time, in the thirties, when tuberculosis was still 'the white plague', regarded by many people with the same irrational horror as AIDS today. One of my earliest childhood memories, dating from my fifth year, is of a hurried departure, after only a night or two, from a luxury Swiss hotel in which, as guests of my well-to-do German grandmother, we had been planning to stay for two weeks. My mother had confided in an English couple, also staying in the hotel, that my father had just come out of a sanatorium. They had passed on this information to some fellow English guests. A deputation had then confronted the manager: it was 'dangerous' to have a TB sufferer scattering his germs about the hotel; either he must go or they would go. The manager, clearly a sensible and decent man, assured them that the director of the sanatorium had told my father, when releasing him, that he was no longer infectious. The guests would not listen. Embarrassed, ashamed, apologetic, the manager asked my father to leave. At the next hotel, my mother was more discreet.

Throughout my childhood, I was always aware of the precarious state of my father's health. A thermometer was not merely a glass tube with mercury in it but a magician's wand, which could wholly transform our previously happy and tranquil lives. 'I'm going to take your temperature,' my mother would say. Impatiently my father would shake his head. 'No, no! I'm all right. I'm perfectly all right.' But my mother, so obdurate where my father's health was concerned even if so yielding to him in all other matters, would insist. I see them now. He is sitting on the edge of his bed or on a chair, the thermometer jutting upwards out of his mouth, as the cigarettes which he chain-smoked similarly jutted. He looks irritable, even petulant. His right leg jigs up and down. My mother frowns down at him, protective and, yes, puzzled, I do not know why. Sometimes, after she has held the thermometer up to the light, she says, with a sigh of relief, 'Nothing' and then begins to shake it vigorously, as though to expunge all memory of those minutes of dread. Sometimes she says: 'Yes, I thought it was up. You can't go to work. I'll send a message to Dr Cameron to come and see you.'

Although death was never mentioned, I seemed to be aware of its inevitability by the time that I was eight or nine. For a few weeks my father was in a sanatorium not in Switzerland but by a lake among the foothills of the Himalayas. My mother, my sister and I – by then my two older sisters were at school in Switzerland – stayed in a nearby farmhouse, the owner of which, a fiercely outspoken, tough but kind widow, took in boarders. Because my father was then deemed to be infectious, only my mother made the trek up the hill to the sanatorium to visit him.

'Why are you leaving us?' I used to demand of her. I was then seven.

'I have to see Daddy.'

'Why can't we come?' my five-year-old sister would ask. 'I want to come, I want to come!' At that she would begin to sob.

189

Either the landlady or her handsome, simple-minded son would then try to distract us – wouldn't we like to look at the newly hatched chickens, see the pigs being fed, play on the swing in the orchard? These prospects rarely consoled us.

My father eventually joined us on the farm. His suit hung on him, the collar of his shirt looked at least two sizes too large. He was tender and affectionate to me as he had rarely been before. I was delighted and yet awed by the change. Leaving my mother and sister behind, we used to go for walks together. 'Not too fast, not too fast!' This former athlete would now soon grow breathless. He would halt and point with his stick. Did I know the name of that mountain over there? And that one? And did I know what bird that was? And the name of that butterfly? He was always eager to educate me; and as with some stern but much loved master, I was terrified of forgetting the lessons learned from him.

Sometimes, motionless except for the shaking of his shoulders, he would start to cough, on and on and on, while with increasing panic, longing to rush away, I would wait for him. Then he would take a small blue bottle out of the pocket of his jacket, unscrew the lid and spit into it. He would screw the lid back. Many years later I read of this kind of bottle in Thomas Mann's *The Magic Mountain* – a 'Blue Peter' it is called in the Lowe-Porter translation.

Not surprisingly tuberculosis filled me with dread for many years, long after the discovery of antibiotics had emptied sanatoria. When, in the sixties, I was living in Japan, I consulted a lung specialist about a persistent cough and loss of weight. Having sounded me thoroughly, he put his head on one side, drew in his breath and then expelled it on a long 'Sah!'. Finally he said 'Maybe tuberculosis.' Couldn't he be sure, one way or another? He shook his head. I must have an X-ray. Now? No, not now, he replied. It was Friday afternoon, I must wait until after the weekend. I passed that weekend in a state of anxiety as acute as if he had told me that he suspected cancer. In the event, there was nothing seriously wrong.

Because of the precariousness of my father's health during my formative years, I have always suffered from undue anxiety about any illness, however trivial, suffered by myself or anyone close to me. Sometimes I see myself laboriously spinning away at my life, as a spider spins away at its web. The web is extraordinarily tensile and tenacious. But some careless passerby can easily rip a hole in it or destroy it altogether. At other times I feel as if life were a matter of picking one's way over the thinnest crust of earth above a sleeping volcano. At any moment, the earth may give way or the volcano erupt.

No doubt it was his illness which made my father suffer from a chronic morbidity; and no doubt my father infected me with that chronic morbidity, though not, mercifully, with the illness itself. When I was eight, he would often take me for walks through the mouldering ruins and the then well-kept grounds of the Residency in Lucknow. It was here that the British had held out with remarkable heroism against the Indians during the Mutiny, later to exact a hideous revenge. There were innumerable tablets commemorating the dead. My father would read their inscriptions to me or, occasionally, make me read them to him. Here was a girl of eleven who had been shot by a sniper. Here was a mother who had been buried, with her two children, aged two and three, under falling masonry. He would point with his stick. 'Now whose grave is that?' If I gave him the correct answer, he was approving: 'Good boy! *Good* boy!' If I gave him the wrong answer or stood in panicky silence, he would cry out impatiently: 'Oh, come on! Come on!'

Sometimes, instead of taking me to the Residency for a walk, he would take me to the cemetery. Some of the gravestones,

particularly those from the nineteenth century, had verses carved
on them. He would know all such verses by heart; and he would
expect me similarly to know them. Anyone who has visited such a
cemetery in India will have been oppressed by the youth of so
many of the people buried in it: girl brides who succumbed to
typhoid, cholera or puerperal fever; subalterns killed by a single
assassin or in some petty skirmish; children dead almost as soon as
they were born. From these graves, as much as from my father's
illness, I received a sense of the ephemerality of human existence.

It was not only disease which threatened my father and so, by
association, also my mother, my sisters and me. One day, in
Allahabad – I must then have been four – my father came home
with red patches on his throat. He spoke in a husky whisper. Two
of his men had dragged some small-time, long-sought gangster
into his office, having arrested him in the bazaar. My father told
them that there was no need to hold the gangster; they should
bring him a chair in which to sit during his interrogation. When
the two policemen let him go, the gangster at once sprang at my
father, gripping his throat with both hands. It was with difficulty
that the two policemen prised him off.

In the hill station of Naini Tal, my father sat down to his usual
luncheon with us. Curry was served; and since he liked his curry
extremely hot, he ate a different one from ours. Luncheon over, he
mounted his horse and, attended by a syce, made his way back
down the hill to his office. Suddenly, he was taken violently ill
outside the house of some friends. He staggered into the house
while the syce, showing admirable presence of mind, mounted the
horse and galloped to the surgery of the doctor to summon his aid.
Those were days when, in India, few private houses possessed
telephones. The doctor managed to save my father's life. So
violent had been the attack that he suspected that poison had been

the cause. This suspicion was confirmed when it was discovered that the cook had vanished, never to reappear or be traced.

Violence of this kind also extended to people close to us. In the hot weather, my father and mother endured a punishing journey across India from Naini Tal to Murree, after learning that the husband of one of my father's sisters, a major in the Indian Army, had been murdered by a sepoy. The murderer had intended to kill not my uncle but another officer, then absent. Why had he wanted to kill the other officer? It was never revealed at the time – there was open talk of promotion denied to the sepoy, there were also whispers of some kind of sexual imbroglio – and I have never been able to discover the truth since. When my father and mother returned to Naini Tal with the distraught young widow and her two little sons, they merely told me that my uncle Billy had died. Although only five, I was precociously already able to read. Some weeks later, thumbing through a copy of the *Illustrated London News*, recently arrived, I saw a picture of my uncle and, with mounting horror, spelled out, word by word, the account of his death. Perhaps my father will also be murdered in the same way, I thought. Perhaps we shall all be murdered.

Once, when we were out for a drive in the car, a hostile crowd suddenly surrounded it, beating on its sides and its bonnet and then, when my father had been obliged to halt it in order not to run anyone over, rocking it from side to side. My father pulled a handful of coins out of his pocket and threw them in a wide arc across the road. The crowd abandoned the car to scavenge for them. My father drove on. I was full of admiration both for his quick-wittedness at the time and for his total composure afterwards.

My father was not merely a man of action; he was also an intellectual. Some years ago, in the course of a lecture at the

English Centre of PEN, Salman Rushdie declared that, in sending out its administrators, England had unloaded on to India 'rubbishy second-raters'. The ignorance of this astounded me. In the years of British rule men who passed out at the top in the Civil Service examinations would often opt for service in India. My godfather had been a Farsi scholar; my father an Urdu one, with in addition a life-long passion for Latin and Greek literature and for English poetry. This passion for English poetry he transmitted to me. I can remember how, on one of our walks, this time on Beachy Head during one of his leaves from India, he suddenly halted and recited into the fierce wind: 'My heart aches and a drowsy numbness pains . . .' I was then eleven, and had already spent three years at private school 'back home'.

From time to time he would set me the task of learning a poem. One of these, a favourite of his and now of mine, was Flecker's *The Old Ships*:

I have seen old ships sail like swans asleep
Beyond the village which men still call Tyre,
With leaden age o'ercargoed, dipping deep
For Famagusta and the hidden sun
Which rings black Cyprus with a lake of fire . . .

I can still hear his voice declaim the poem; I can still myself recite it from beginning to end.

At the time I was often resentful at thus being obliged, not merely at my private school but even during holidays with my parents, to learn poetry by heart. Now I am grateful, and sorry for the pupils of today, in general absolved from all such rote learning. What my father forced me to learn, often irritably correcting me as I recited it to him – 'No, no, not "*Will* I compare thee to a summer's day?" – shall, shall, *shall*' – has remained with me, like some invisible trust fund, on which I have been always able to draw in need. The importance of such an invisible trust fund was brought home to me when I was International President of PEN. Repeatedly writers who had spent years in prison, with little or no access to books, told me how they had recited either to themselves or to their fellow prisoners poetry which they had learned in their youth. It had been an unfailing support to them, as, in circumstances far less dire, it has been an unfailing support to me.

My father's own father had forced him to learn by heart passages in Latin from the *Aeneid* when he was only five. This grandfather of mine had been a judge in Madras. In his early fifties, still a bachelor, he retired, returned to Europe, and there married the daughter, only eighteen years old, of an impoverished German aristocrat. Somehow, during his years in India, he had become rich. How? I have never been able to discover. Did he brilliantly invest his savings? Or, as a judge, did he find other, less reputable means of accumulating money? Within some twenty years, travelling in his retirement about Europe, he had fathered a dozen children. Since he treated my father with all the severity of a Victorian paterfamilias – making him endure daily cold baths at an early age, beating him for the smallest trangression – it is to my father's credit that the only severity which he ever showed me was a verbal one. Cousins, a girl and a boy, often used to come and stay with us. When the cousins, along with my sister and myself, were discovered in some wrong-doing, their otherwise equable father, a railway engineer, or their formidable mother, my mother's oldest sister, would beat them; but neither my father nor my mother would ever lay a hand on my sister and myself. Only once, exasperated beyond endurance because I insisted on making a noise when he was trying to listen to a Beethoven quartet on the wind-up gramophone, my father pulled off his slipper and whacked my behind three times with it. I was far too amazed to feel any pain.

It is difficult now to convey that, by the standards of his time, my father was the same sort of liberal as his friend Malcolm Darling, often said to be the prototype for Fielding in E.M. Forster's *A Passage to India*, or Malcolm Hailey (later Lord Hailey), Governor of the United Provinces for much of the period of my father's service there. My father would freely use phrases such as 'wog', 'black as your boots' and 'a touch of the tar-brush'. I can remember him once reciting a limerick – whether of his own authorship or someone else's I do not know – over a luncheon table in a restaurant and how we all, children, aunts and uncles, laughed uproariously at it:

> There was a young man of Sydenham
> Who lost his best pants with a quid in them.
> He found them again
> Down Petticoat Lane,
> But there wasn't a quid but a Yid in them.

Yet, unlike the majority of his colleagues, he was interested in the art and literature of India and he had many Indian friends. One of these friends, a Christian whose brother-in-law was the first Governor of Bombay after Independence, became my godmother.

When I was thirteen, in the year before his death, my father found me reading Christopher Isherwood's *Mr Norris Changes Trains* and took it away from me. It was 'wonderfully entertaining pornography', he said, but I was neither young enough nor old enough to read it. This last remark illustrated his often expressed belief that pornography had no deleterious effect on either children or adults, but only on adolescents. Needless to say, I procured another copy of Isherwood's novel, which I read in secret. The only effect it had on me was a beneficial one: it gave me an early literary lesson in the use of irony and the merits of concision. Oddly, my father also forbad me to read Warwick Deeping's best-selling *Sorrel and Son* – 'it's pornography and it's tripe, and I won't have you reading either.' Today, most people would agree with only the second of these objections to the book.

My father had both a love and an admiration for Kipling, whom (in common with many Indians) he believed to have understood India and the Indians far better than E.M. Forster. He transmitted this love and admiration to me. When I was a precocious child of eight, due within a few weeks to be sent back 'home' to be educated, I was browsing in my father's library and so somehow came on the story, *Baa, Baa, Black Sheep*, about Kipling's sufferings when, a remittance child such as I myself was about to become, he was boarded with a family in England. I was filled with apprehension, even terror. But fortunately the relatives who took charge of me, although sometimes negligent or impatient, were never unkind.

When the time came to send her children back to England, my mother, like most other English mothers in India at that period, was confronted with a terrible dilemma. Was she to accompany them and make a home for them; or was she to stay with her husband? My mother decided (and I am sure that she was right) to stay with her husband. The wife of one of my father's colleagues was travelling back to England at the same time and I was therefore placed in her charge for the long sea voyage. My mother had planned to accompany us on the train from Lucknow to Bombay but then abandoned the idea, since my father was once more ill. That she should opt to stay with him, rather than come to see me off on the ship, filled me with anger and grief. As, late at night, the train moved out of the station, my mother, clutching my hand, ran beside it. I felt that eventually, so strong was her grasp, either I should be yanked out of the carriage or my arm would be severed. Finally, at the end of the platform, she let go. I have no memory of whether my father was at the station or not. Presumably he was too ill to be there. Something of my anger and grief remained with me. She had abandoned me for him. He would always be her first choice.

I had always been a mother's boy, perhaps inevitably since my father was so often absent because of either illness or the work which he took so seriously. If I was jealous of my father, I think that he was also jealous of me, resenting it if my mother made too much fuss over me ('Oh, stop worrying about the boy! He's only got a common cold'), spent too much time with me ('Do hurry up! We're going to be late yet again'), or was too generous to me ('What's the use of giving him a watch like that? He'll only break it'). It was over my mother's absence, not my father's, that, alone in the cabin which I shared with the wife of my father's colleague, I wept secret, scalding tears; and when, from school in England, I wrote letters beginning 'Darling Mummy and Daddy', it was really only to my mother that I was speaking.

I was thirteen when my father spent his last leave in England. To his and my own delight, I had just won a scholarship to Harrow. Then, all at once, he told me that he had decided that Harrow was not the right school for me. He wished me to go to Shrewsbury instead. Since among public schools Harrow was then regarded as second only to Eton, I was at first astounded and then furious. Why, why, why? I demanded. My father explained. Even more than Eton, Harrow catered for the sons of rich fathers. He was not a rich father, and I should therefore feel at a constant disadvantage. I protested loudly and then, when that failed to change his mind, I sulked. Now, in retrospect, I see that he was right. At my private school, most of the boys were the sons of rich fathers. On Parents' Days, we all used to sit on the wall which separated the school grounds from the road and watch the Rolls Royces, Bentleys, Daimlers and Armstrong Siddeleys arriving. When one of my uncles turned up in an ancient two-seater Morris Cowley with a dickey, an ironic cheer went up. I was deeply ashamed.

During that last leave, much of it spent in Hereford, my father yet again fell ill and had to go into hospital in London to have an operation. It was typical of his gallows humour that he should be delighted to find that the three medical men in charge of him were called Cutler, Ripman and De'Ath. Refusing a lengthy conval-escence, he boarded the P. & O. liner to return to India on the date originally fixed. My mother and two elder sisters, now grown up, were with him. My sisters told me that he was in the highest of spirits, amusing and charming everyone with whom he came into contact. (Long after his death, people who had known him, would say one of two things about him to me. The first was: He was such fun. The second was: He was such wonderful company.) Then, on board a small motor-boat that was taking passengers ashore at Port Said, he began to cough on the thick, black fumes belching out from the ancient engine and suddenly had a haemorrhage. Although he reached India, he died soon after.

By then I had started my first term at Shrewsbury. Since it was thought that anxiety over my father would make it even more difficult for me to settle down, this last illness was concealed from me. Yet I knew, knew with absolute certainty, even while I was struggling to come to terms with the ferocious discipline of Shrewsbury in the early thirties, that far away, in that now remote part of the world, a lost paradise which had once been so familiar to me, my father was dying. Because of that certainty and despite efforts of rationalist friends to convince me otherwise – my father had been seriously ill, it was natural enough that I should have anticipated his death, they tell me – I have always had an unshakeable belief in extra-sensory perception.

I was undressing for bed, when a monitor entered the dormitory and told me that the housemaster wished to see me in his study. 'I wonder what you've done,' he gloated, clearly supposing that I was being summoned for a beating. I pulled on the clothes which I had just taken off. So it's happened, I thought, with a bleak composure. It's happened.

The housemaster, a decent, unemotional, inarticulate bachelor, clearly dreaded his task.

'I'm afraid I've some bad news for you,' he said when, with unusual gentleness, he had told me to sit down.

I nodded.

'I expect you knew that your father had been ill. Very ill. Very *very* ill.'

He paused, reaching for a silver cigarette box on the table between us and momentarily holding it out to me before hurriedly withdrawing it and himself extracting a cigarette.

Again I nodded.

'Well – I'm afraid – I'm afraid I have to tell you . . . He's died.'

Yet again I nodded.

He stared at me in a wondering disbelief. Perhaps I had not taken in what he had told me? 'You'll miss him. Of course you'll miss him. But you must be brave – for your mother's sake.'

This last was something that my relatives, who came to visit me in Shrewsbury in the days that followed, also repeatedly told me. It puzzled me. Why could one not be brave merely for one's own sake?

Eventually the housekeeper, also unusually gentle, arrived to take me to the guest-room in which it was agreed that I should sleep that night. She looked at me with the same wondering disbelief as the housemaster had done. I was still totally composed. I had shed not a tear.

'I expect you'd like a hot-water bottle,' she said. 'And I'm going to bring you a mug of Ovaltine. A hot drink is always comforting, isn't it?'

I thought of the freezing dormitory, its windows open by decree, however cold the weather. I was glad not to be in it.

In bed, I hugged the hot-water bottle to me. Then, as though its warmth were at long last thawing out something frozen within me, I began first to snuffle and then to sob. I must eventually have been overheard by the housemaster and the housekeeper. I could hear their voices in the passageway.

'He's crying,' the housemaster said. 'Do you think we ought . . .?'

'Crying will be good for him,' she replied, wiser than he. 'Let's leave him to it.'

Eventually I fell asleep, to wake, in the small hours, to find my bed damp and cold. For a horrified moment I thought that I had wet it. Then I realised that the bottle had leaked. I tried to go to sleep again but could not do so. Shivering I got up, dragged a blanket and the eiderdown off the bed, and went over to an armchair by the window. Intermittently I dozed.

When the housekeeper arrived with a cup of tea and two biscuits, she surveyed the bed and the chair.

'I'm afraid I had an accident,' I said.

She looked momentarily cross. Then she said: 'Oh, don't worry!' Clearly she assumed that I had wet the bed.

'It was the hot-water bottle. It leaked.'

'Oh, gosh! Oh, golly! It's not been used for donkey's years. Oh, I *am* sorry! How awful for you.'

My grief for my father was real; it was also deep. But then, as that winter term dragged on, an emotion even more real and even deeper coalesced with it. This was guilt. From time to time, in the weeks while my father was dying at the house of my uncle and aunt in Ratlam, I had sometimes mused on the changes which would occur in my life and in the lives of my mother and my sisters after he had gone. My mother would come to England, she would make a home for us, we should all be happy together. Later, all these things happened. My mother did, indeed, return to England; previously dependent on innumerable servants, she did indeed make a home for us on the cruelly diminished income which her pension provided; and we were indeed happy – I far, far happier than I had been during those years of being a remittance child in charge of relatives or friends of the family, and as happy as I have ever been since. Reflecting on how in my musings I had anticipated all the changes which would follow on the death of my father, I began to persuade myself that somehow I had caused that death merely by thinking about it. The guilt intensified. It became almost unbearable. Years later, when I spoke of this guilt to a psychiatrist friend, he told me that he often encountered it among his patients. One of them, a middle-aged spinster, had even attempted suicide after her invalid mother, whom she had selflessly tended for many years, eventually died. The spinster had persuaded herself that, because in her darkest hours she had thought 'Oh, if only she would *go*!' she had somehow hastened that going.

Throughout my life I have often wondered how different would have been my life if, instead of dying of tuberculosis, my father had recovered from it. I should have passed my school and university years in greater affluence; and I should no doubt have initially felt less ill at ease in a man's world if he had been on hand to do such things as introduce me to his tailor, arrange for me to become a member of his club, and speak to the right people when I embarked on a career. But our relationship would certainly not have been wholly easy. I have no doubt that, just as he took pride and pleasure in my scholastic achievements, he would have gone on doing so. Himself a thwarted writer – from time to time he would contribute light verse to such papers in India as the *Times of India*, the *Pioneer* and the *Statesman* – he would also have been delighted that I eventually achieved some success as a novelist. But, unlike my mother, he would have been appalled by my extreme left-wing views in my youth, and by my refusal to join the Officers Training Corps at Shrewsbury and my subsequent conscientious objection to the War.

Even more he would have been appalled by my homosexuality – of which, I suspect, he had a disquieting prescience, in the manner of fathers and mothers, even in my early youth. 'Take your hand off your hip! Anyone would think you were a nancy boy,' he chided me once. At my seventh birthday party, he crept up behind me with a cracker and pulled it over my neck. When I burst into admittedly unnecessary tears – I had felt no pain, only shock – he had exclaimed in disgust 'Oh, for God's sake! What's the matter with you? You're not a *girl*!' Yet though so perspicacious about my sexuality, he could also be strangely innocent. When we were staying in Eastbourne – I was then eleven – one of my father's friends, a retired Indian Army colonel, a bachelor, began to take an inordinate interest in me. I was uneasily aware, despite a lack of sexual knowledge such as few boys of that age would suffer from today, that there was something wrong with the relationship. But as the colonel bought me sweets and books, treated me to ice-creams in cafés on the front, took me swimming, took me to the cinema, my father seemed totally unaware of what was going on. 'I don't want to go out with him,' I would say, unable to explain, since I did not know, why I felt this; and my father would then say something like 'Don't be a little ass! You want to go swimming, don't you? I'm far too busy to take you. Go on – go, go, go!'

In the years that followed my father's death, I replaced him with three other fathers in turn. The first of these was a young science master at Shrewsbury, Humphrey Moore, who almost daily invited me over to his rooms, who encouraged me to write, and who, himself a poet, introduced me to Yeats, Auden and, in translation, Rilke. As a writer I owe more to him than to anyone else in my life. He was, of course, a pederast; but he never made any sexual approach to me. When, a few years ago, I learned of his death, a wave of grief swept over me – even though I had never seen him after leaving school. My second surrogate father was Harold Nicolson. Since his death he has tended to receive at best a condescending and at worst a hostile press. But in his magnanimity, his tolerance, his essential decency, he struck me as the model of what I should myself try to be. The last of these surrogate fathers was the novelist C.H.B. (Clifford) Kitchin, so unlike myself in his loftily fastidious, damn-you-all eccentricity founded on great wealth.

Four years ago I decided to travel out to India to visit my father's grave. My mother, now a hundred-and-one, spoke to me of it: 'It's in this cemetery on a hillside. It's such a beautiful place. You cannot imagine. There are hills all around it, green hills even when the weather is hottest, and it's all so peaceful, unbelievably peaceful.'

It was dusk when my travelling companion, Diana Petre, and I approached Ratlam in our hired car. The outskirts of the town were squalid beyond words. There were stark factories, the smoke from their chimneys staining the sky a bilious yellow, and all around them there were sheds, little more than hutches, constructed out of wood, cardboard and corrugated iron. 'How hideous it all is!' I exclaimed; and almost at the same time Diana pointed excitedly and cried out: 'There! There it is! There!'

I could only just decipher the battered sign on the wall: Protestant Cemetery.

Diana and I clambered out of the car; then, with her usual tact, she wandered off, away from me, leaving me to find the grave alone. The grass was yellow and dusty. In the distance, a small boy was striking out with a stick at the rumps of a herd of emaciated cows, their udders swinging as they bucked and skittered away from him.

I found the grave. The grass had been cut around it. The stone was in place and free of moss. Later, I was to learn that Eurasian Christians from a nearby church still tended the place.

I stared at the grave. I felt the tears coming, unexpected, to my eyes. One ran down to my mouth. I tasted its salt.

Strangely, I felt nearer to my father then in his death than at any time during his life.

When I returned to England, the first thing that my mother asked me was whether I had visited the grave. Yes, I said, yes, I had visited it.

'Isn't that a perfect spot?'

'Yes, perfect. Absolutely perfect.'

AUTHORS' NOTES

DAVID SIMON was born in London in 1958 of Grenadian parents. He has had two novels published and was writer-in-residence at the University of Warwick in 1987. In 1990 he won the Peterloo Open Poetry Competition. He is the founder of Ebony Supplementary Saturday School and currently teaches English at Brixton College.

JOHN FOWLES is the author of several bestselling novels, including *The French Lieutenant's Woman*, *The Magus*, *The Collector* and *Ebony Tower*, as well as works of non-fiction. He has long been concerned over nature, not excluding the human side of it.

DAVID EPSTEIN has written plays which have been produced in New York and across the United States. He has written for public television and network television in the United States and is currently writing a screenplay for David Puttnam.

CHRISTOPHER RAWLENCE is a writer, film-maker and librettist. His films include *The Missing Reel*, *About Time* and *The Man Who Mistook His Wife for a Hat*. His books include *About Time* (1985) and *The Missing Reel* (1990). His previous careers include founder/actor/writer/director for Red Ladder Theatre and Lecturer in Art History at University College, London. Among his interests are: observing brown trout in clear Hampshire chalk streams; recognising civil aviation engines by ear; and picking up stray playing cards in the street.

JOHN McVICAR is a writer and commentator on law and order issues.

JOHN HOYLAND works variously as a writer, editor, TV researcher and campaign organiser. He has published a children's novel, *The Ivy Garland*, and is co-author with Jonathan Chadwick of two plays. He works currently for *New Scientist*.

PAUL ATKINSON was involved in socialism and men's sexual politics in the 1970s, and was a member of the Achilles Heel Collective. His contributions to the magazine have been published in *The Achilles Heel Reader*. He works as an analytical psychotherapist in private practice in London.

FRANCIS KING was born in Switzerland and brought up in India. He published his first three novels while still an undergraduate at Oxford. He then spent sixteen years working abroad for the British Council, before leaving to devote himself full-time to writing. He has won a number of literary prizes, including the Somerset Maugham Prize, the Katherine Mansfield Short Story Prize and the Yorkshire Post Novel of the Year Award. His most recent fiction is the novella *Secret Lives*.